INTRODUCTION TO THE ENGLISH LEGAL SYSTEM

REVISION GUIDE

GW00392863

INTRODUCTION TO THE ENGLISH LEGAL SYSTEM

REVISION GUIDE

DR ÖZGÜR HEVAL ÇINAR

TRANSNATIONAL PRESS LONDON

2021

Law Series: 2

INTRODUCTION TO THE ENGLISH LEGAL SYSTEM – REVISION GUIDE

By Dr Özgür Heval Çınar

Copyright © 2021 Transnational Press London

First Published in 2021 by TRANSNATIONAL PRESS LONDON in the United Kingdom, 12 Ridgeway Gardens, London, N6 5XR, UK.

www.tplondon.com

Transnational Press London® and the logo and its affiliated brands are registered trademarks.

Requests for permission to reproduce material from this work should be sent to: admin@tplondon.com

Paperback
ISBN: 978-1-912997-76-3
Digital
ISBN: 978-1-912997-68-8

Cover Design: Nihal Yazgan

www.tplondon.com

CONTENTS

ABBREVIATIONS

AC: Law Reports, Appeal Cases

ADR: Alternative Dispute Resolution

All ER: All England Law Reports

BCC: British Company Law Cases

BCLC: Butterworths Company Law Cases

BMLR: Butterworths Medico-Legal Reports

CA: Court of Appeal

CrPR: Criminal Procedure Rules

Cr App R: Criminal Appeal Reports

Crim LR: Criminal Law Review

CoE: Council of Europe

Ch: Law Reports, Chancery Division

CJEU: Court of Justice of the European Union

CL: Current Law

CLI: Current Legal Information

CLJ: Cambridge Law Journal

CLP: Current Legal Problems

CLR: Commonwealth Law Reports

CMLR: Common Market Law Reports

CMLRev: Common Market Law Review

Conv: Conveyancer and Property Lawyer

CPR: Civil Procedure Rules

Cr App Rep: Criminal Appeal Reports

Crim L Rev: Criminal Law Review

Crim LQ: Criminal Law Quarterly

DJ: District Judge - County Court

EAT: Employment Appeal Tribunal

ECA: European Communities Act

ECHR: European Convention on Human Rights

ECtHR: European Court of Human Rights

ECJ: European Court of Justice

EG: Estates Gazette

EHRR: European Human Rights Reports

EHRLR: European Human Rights Law Review

ELJ: European Law Journal

ELRev: European Law Review

Env LR: Environmental Law Reports

ER: English Reports

EWCA Civ: England and Wales Court of Appeal, Civil Division

EWCA Crim: England and Wales Court of Appeal, Criminal Division

EWHC (Admin): England and Wales High Court (Administrative Court)

EWHC (Fam): England and Wales High Court (Family Division)

EWHC (Ch): England and Wales High Court (Chancery Division)

EWCH (Comm): England and Wales High Court (Commercial Court)

EWCH (Pat): England and Wales High Court (Patents Court)

EWHC (QB): England and Wales High Court (Queen's Bench Division)

Fam: Law Reports, Family Division

FLR: Family Law Reports

FCR: Family Court Reporter

FPR: Family Procedure Rules

HRA: Human Rights Act

HRLR: Human Rights Law Reports

INGOs: International Non-governmental Organisations

IRLR: Industrial Relations Law Reports

J: Mr Justice - High Court

JBL: Journal of Business Law

J Crim L: Journal of Criminal Law

JCPC: The Judicial Committee of the Privy Council

JP: Justice of the Peace Reports

KB: King's Bench

KIR: Knight's Industrial Reports

LC: Lord Chancellor

LCJ: Lord Chief Justice

LJ: Lord Justice – Court of Appeal

Lloyd's Rep: Lloyd's Law Reports

LQR: Law Quarterly Review

LSG: Law Society Gazette

LGLR: Local Government Law Reports

MR: Master of the Rolls

MLR: Modern Law Review

NLJ: New Law Journal

OJ: Official Journal of the European Union

OJLS: Oxford Journal of Legal Studies

P: President. Head of Family Division and President of QB Division

PC: Judicial Committee of the Privy Council

PL: Public Law

QB: Queen's Bench

QC: Queen's Counsel

SIs: Statutory Instruments

SJ: Solicitors' Journal

SLT: Scots' Law Times

SLR: Student Law Review

TLR: Times Law Reports

UK: United Kingdom

UKHRR: United Kingdom Human Rights Reports

UKPC: United Kingdom Privy Council

UKSC: United Kingdom Supreme Court

UKHL: United Kingdom House of Lords

UN: United Nations

WLR: Weekly Law Reports

YB Eur L: Yearbook of European Law

ABOUT THE AUTHOR

Dr Özgür Heval Çınar is a lawyer. Presently, he is an associate professor at the University of Greenwich, School of Law and Criminology. He completed his PhD at the School of Law, University of Essex. Previously, he was a post-doc fellow at the University of Oxford between 2012-2016.

FOREWORD

The English Legal System is a legal system that dates back to 1066, evolving over time until the present day. Throughout the world, it is known as common law. While common law consists of case-law and statutes, it has reached its present state by incorporating elements of international law, prerogative power and non-legal sources such as conventions and customs.

When it is considered that the United Kingdom (UK) has three separate jurisdictions – those in England and Wales; Scotland and Northern Ireland – this subject takes on a more interesting and complicated state. Hence, all three jurisdictions have their own laws, court structures, lawyers and judges. Nevertheless, laws valid in one jurisdiction, especially those originating from legislation (Acts of Parliament and Statutory Instruments) may have equal, or very similar force, in the other two jurisdictions. Moreover, although courts may hand down different judgments in cases, depending on the jurisdiction, the UK Supreme Court is the highest court for all three jurisdictions. This book will closely examine the legal system of England and Wales in particular, while endeavouring to take a close look at the other jurisdictions at intervals.

Besides this, the UK was a member of the European Union (EU) between 1973 and 2020 and adapted its legal system to EU standards. However, it is still not clear how the UK's relationship will be with the EU anymore after it officially withdrew its membership on 31 January 2020 even though the Trade and Cooperation Agreement was signed by the EU and the UK on 30 December 2020. Furthermore, it was one of the first countries to sign and ratify the European Convention on Human Rights that came into force in 1953, following which it enacted the Human Rights Act in 1998, recognising the rights and freedoms embodies in the Convention in an effective way, shaping the English Legal System and rendering it even more complicated.

Hence, the reason for the emergence of this book is that other publications do not explain such a complex issue in plain language, which makes it very difficult for those taking an interest, in particular A-level as well as LLB/LLM law students. Moreover, the experience of teaching this course for many years and particularly knowing the fields in which students experience difficulties, made me aware of the need for such a work. This book does not repeat material that is available in many textbooks that are in print. Rather, it endeavours to present every topic in plain language and concludes every chapter with a fictitious explanatory sample case. In other words, it is an introduction to the subject of the English Legal System, the objective of which is to explain the topic both theoretically and in its application. Additionally, this book will assist students to prepare for courseworks/examinations. At the end of the book, there is also a test that summarises all the subjects contained in the book, which is appropriate to the first stage SQE examination model that will be introduced on 1 September 2021. I hope this book will help all those who have an interest in this subject.

I would also like to express my gratitude to all those at Transnational Press London who provided their full support, and to Prof İbrahim Sirkeci, Mr Andrew Penny, Ms Hülya Ak and to others who contributed that I am unable to name individually here.

Dr Özgür Heval Çınar

CHAPTER I

INTRODUCTION: HISTORY, SOURCES AND INSTITUTIONS

Learning Outcomes:

In this chapter, you should be able to understand:

- ✓ the functions of law;
- ✓ English legal history and the development of common law;
- ✓ the nature and role of equity and how it relates to the common law;
- ✓ the impact of the Judicature Acts.

Questions and Answers:

1-) What is law? What are the functions of the law?

According to the Cambridge English Dictionary, the law means "the system of rules of a particular country, group, or area of activity."[1]

The law has many functions. One of these is to uphold peace and security in a society; the law administers relationships between individuals and/or entities and/or public authorities; it safeguards fundamental rights and freedoms and enables the unhindered functioning of economic life and political activities. The law also has to evolve as societal norms change so that it is still relevant to citizens, while retaining the above functions.[2]

2-) Who is subject to law?

Only legal persons are affected by law. They may be in two forms:

- – A natural person such as human beings;
- – An artificial person (also known as juridical person) such as corporations, firms, government agencies.

---

[1] Cambridge Dictionary, 'Law', https://dictionary.cambridge.org/dictionary/english/law (accessed 1 February 2021).
[2] BPP Law School, *Study Notes on English Legal System*, BPP Law School, 2018, p. 2.

3-) What are the different types of law?

Law can be codified under different types of law.

Public Law	Private Law
The law regarding the relationship between the individual and the state such as constitutional and administrative law.	The law regarding the relationship between the individual and other legal persons such as contract law, tort law, property law and company law. The state is not a part of the legal issue.

Criminal Law	Civil Law
• Criminal law is part of public law. • A crime is seen as an offence against the community (it is in the public interest for anti-social behavior to be prevented). • The State will prosecute the defendant. Prosecutions that conclude in the conviction of the accused for a crime lead to punishment. This may be a fine, a prison sentence, or, on occasions, both. • The standard of proof is beyond reasonable doubt.	• Civil law is part of private law. • A civil wrong is a private matter to be resolved between the private parties. • Claimant brings an action/sues the defendant. For example, the defendant in a case of tort or breach of contract may have to pay damages to the injured party, or be subjected to an injunction, with which they will be required to comply. • The standard of proof is on the balance of probabilities.

4-) What are the legal systems?

There are two main legal systems in the world: Civil and Common Law.[3]

Civil Law (also known as 'continental system')	Common Law
Civil law is a system based on the supremacy of written laws. It is codified, meaning that judges merely interpret laws introduced by the legislature. The previous decisions of judges are persuasive, but not binding. For instance, France, Germany and Turkey have civil law systems.	Common law consists of statutory and case law (binding judicial precedent). Moreover, the English legal system is referred to as a common law system. In addition, there are several other countries that have a common law system such as Canada, Australia and New Zealand.
Most civil law systems function on the basis of an inquisitorial approach. This entails a judge carrying out an investigation by asking questions to witnesses. The counsel (lawyer) makes sure that the judge complies with procedural rules.	Most common law systems, including that in the UK, use an adversarial approach involving two or more opposing sides with an independent judge as arbiter. The role of the judge is to ensure that both sides (e.g. *claimant v defendant*) adhere to procedural rules. Both sides are allowed to call and examine witnesses.

5-) Why do you study the 'English legal system' rather than the 'United Kingdom (UK) legal system'?

The reason is 'devolution'. England is an essential country of the United Kingdom of Great Britain and Northern Ireland alongside Wales, Scotland and Northern Ireland. That is, powers have been allocated that permit each country to frame laws in certain areas. In the event of conflict between UK laws and laws of one of the countries that make up the UK, the UK law has supremacy.[4]

Wales does not have a separate legal system because of the Laws of Wales Act 1535 and 1543. It means that the laws of England apply in Wales.

Scotland and Northern Ireland have separate legal systems. But an Act of the UK Parliament is still applicable in these countries. For instance,

---

[3] Gillespie, A. and Weare, S., *The English Legal System*, 5th ed., Oxford University Press, 2015, pp. 12-15.
[4] Thomas, M. and McGourlay, C., *Concentrate English Legal System*, Oxford University Press, 2017, p. 4.

Scotland is not able to legislate on matters which are reserved such as the constitution, foreign affairs, defence, international development, immigration and nationality.[5]

6-) What is the historical development of the English Legal System?

There are four important eras:[6]

1) **Pre-1066**: No unitary legal system. In that period, England was a country consisting of different tribes in regions that became kingdoms. These entities all had their own rules to maintain order. There were several local courts such as Shire and Hundred courts.

2) **1066-1485**: England became a feudal nation. A centralised system of justice was constructed with the King at its centre. Hence, the King's Courts were created, with various 'branches' of the court such as the Court of Exchequer (dealing with royal finances); the Court of Common Pleas (dealing with land law issues); the Court of King's Bench (dealing with criminal law issues). Local courts (Assizes Courts) were later on developed dealing with mainly criminal law matters.

3) **1485-1832**: Equity law was developed because litigants who considered they were not obtaining justice in the King's Courts began to appeal to the King to mete out justice in their cases. Equity means that 'the conscience of the King'. By petitioning the King redress could be sought for perceived lack of justice. The King had the judicial power to rule in such cases. The King handed over the responsibility for dealing with these petitions to the Chancellor. At that time the Chancellor was usually a religious figure. By the end of the 15th century the Chancery evolved into the Court of Chancery, which had judicial powers. The Court of Chancery became a court of conscience to counterbalance the shortcomings of the common law system. Equity rules changed according to who was Chancellor until the end of the 16th century.[7]

As the equity system grew it began to compete with common law. Litigants found equity rules could be used to obtain an injunction to prevent the enforcement of a common law order.[8] The Common Law Procedure Act of 1854 enabled common law courts to hand down equitable remedies. The Chancery Amendment Act of 1858 endowed the Court of Chancery with

---

[5] 'Guidance Devolution Settlement: Scotland', https://www.gov.uk/guidance/devolution-settlement-scotland#interaction-between-devolved-and-reserved-matters (accessed 1 February 2021).
[6] 'The English Legal System', http://prezi.com/0ojce5qz9jr1/the-english-legal-system (accessed 1 February 2021).
[7] Cockburn, T. and Shirley, M., *Nutshell: Equity*, 5th ed., Thomson Reuters (Lawbook Co)., 2019.
[8] *Co-op Insurance v. Argyll Stores* [1997] 3 All ER 297.

the power to award damages instead of an equitable remedy. Nevertheless, friction between the two systems of law persisted.[9]

4) 1832 to the present day: The following key Acts should be taken into account.

- ✓ County Courts Act 1846: Re-organisation of local courts;
- ✓ Common Law Procedure Act 1854: Power to grant equitable remedies;
- ✓ Judicature Acts 1873-1875: Creation of one civil court system;
- ✓ European Communities Act (ECA 1972); Human Rights Act (HRA 1998): European mechanism started influencing the domestic law in 20th century;
- ✓ House of Lords was replaced by Supreme Court. Moreover, other radical changes were made in Constitutional Reform Act (CRA 2005) and in Supreme Court Act 2009. **?**

7-) What are the fundamental principles in the English Legal System?

- ✓ **Rule of Law:** This encompasses three basic rules:

  1) It signifies the supremacy of regular law over arbitrary power;
  2) It means everyone is equal before the law;
  3) It entails the constitution being the ordinary law of the land, where individual rights are safeguarded by common law, not by a written constitutional document.[10]

- ✓ **Doctrine of constitutionalism:** This is a doctrine which considers a government's legitimacy is determined by a constitution, which is based on "conformity with broad philosophical values within a state."[11]

- ✓ **Separation of powers:** The doctrine of separation of powers provides that there are three essential functions (the legislature, the executive and the judiciary) in the administration of an independent state.

- ✓ **Supremacy of parliament:** This encompasses three basic rules:

  1) Parliament is the supreme law-making body;
  2) No Parliament may be bound by a predecessor or may bind a successor;

---

[9] BPP, p. 9.
[10] Dicey, A. V., *Introduction to the Study of the Law of Constitution*, Liberty Fund Inc., 2019.
[11] Barnett, H., *Constitutional and Administrative Law*, 10th ed., Routledge, 2013, p. 5.

3) No person or body may question the validity of an enactment of Parliament.[12]

✓ **Ministerial responsibility (individual and collective):** Government ministers are considered accountable for whatever their department does, in principle and, generally, in practice.[13]

✓ **Representative democracy:** This is a form of democracy based on the principle of people electing candidates and parties to represent them.[14]

✓ **Effective judicial review of executive action:** Courts use a mechanism called judicial review to examine decision-making processes and the legality or otherwise of the actions or decisions of public bodies.[15]

✓ **Judicial independence:** Judicial independence is of the utmost importance for the concept of the separation of powers and the rule of law. If the judiciary is not independent and is subject to improper influence, then genuine separation of powers cannot exist and it is not possible to hold the government to account in a satisfactory manner. Article 6 of the European Convention on Human Rights - ECHR (Article 6 of HRA 1998) states that "…everyone is entitled to a fair and public hearing within a reasonable time by an independent and impartial tribunal established by law…"

In the UK there are significant protections to ensure the judiciary maintains its independence and impartiality:

Tenure: Security of tenure is enshrined in the Senior Courts Act 1981, Section 11 (formerly the Supreme Court Act 1981) for Crown Court, High Court and Court of Appeal judges, while the tenure of judges in the Supreme Court is protected in the CRA 2005, Section 33. These two Acts state that judges hold their office 'during good behaviour' and may only be removed by the monarch after an address has been submitted by both Houses of Parliament.

Immunity: Judges have immunity from lawsuit regarding any acts while carrying out their judicial function, even if they make a mistake. This includes the law of defamation. Hence, judges are able to reach

---

[12] Dicey, *Introduction to the Study of the Law of Constitution*.

[13] 'Guidance Ministerial Code', https://www.gov.uk/government/publications/ministerial-code (accessed 1 February 2021).

[14] Crick, B., *Democracy: A Very Short Introduction*, Oxford University Press, 2002.

[15] Harris, P.; Hurden, N. and the Constitutional and Administrative Law Team, *GDL & LLM Study Notes on Constitutional and Administrative Law*, BPP Law School, 2018, p. 206.

decisions independently without outside pressure. While judges in the higher courts have absolute immunity, the situation in the lower courts is not quite so straightforward.

Open courts: It is an important principle that trials take place in courts that are open to the public, in order that justice is seen to be done. Trials only take place behind closed doors, 'in camera', in the event that an open court hearing might prevent justice being done or due to the need to protect vulnerable people.

Political independence: Full-time judges are not allowed to become MPs and are expected to be apolitical. Similarly, members of the government should avoid commenting on decisions reached by judges. This principle is not always followed. This also means that courts have no jurisdiction over proceedings in Parliament.

Judicial appointments: The Judicial Appointments Commission was established by Section 6 of the CRA 2005. The aim of this act was to enhance the administration of justice and strengthen public confidence in the system of justice. Section 63 of this act emphasises that judicial appointments must be based on merit and good character alone.

Head of the Judiciary: Following the introduction of the CRA 2005, Section 7, the Lord Chief Justice replaced the Lord Chancellor as the Head of the Judiciary. Consequently, the office is no longer under direct political control.[16]

---

[16] Harris and others, pp. 42-43.

CHAPTER II

SOURCES OF LAW I: DOMESTIC LEGISLATION

Learning Outcomes:

In this chapter, you should be able to understand:

- ✓ the difference between primary and secondary legislation;
- ✓ the law-making process;
- ✓ the different approaches to statutory interpretation.

Questions and Answers:

1-) What are the primary and secondary sources in the English Legal System?

Primary Sources	Secondary Sources
• Acts of Parliament (primary legislation) • Statutory Instruments (secondary legislation) • Byelaws (secondary legislation) • Procedural Rules (secondary legislation) • Orders in Council (secondary legislation) • Decisions of superior courts (case law) • EU and International Law • Royal Prerogatives • Conventions • Customs	• Books including text books • Peer-reviewed or non-referred articles in law journals

2-) What types of legislation are there in England and Wales?

Primary Legislation	Secondary Legislation (also known as Delegated Legislation)

Acts of Parliament. There are two kinds:
  • **Private (Personal) Act;**
  • **Public (General) Act.**
	• Statutory Instruments;
	• Byelaws;
	• Procedural Rules;
	• Orders in Council.

3-) Explain Acts of Parliament

An Act of Parliament is a document containing legislation voted on and passed by Parliament.

There are two types of Acts of Parliament, private Acts and public Acts. A private (or personal) Act of Parliament confers powers or benefits on particular places or people. An example is the Transport for London Act 2016.

As for Public (or general) Acts, they are Acts which confer powers or benefits on public concern in general. The ECA 1972 or HRA 1998 are examples.[1]

4-) Explain secondary (delegated) legislation

Secondary (also known as delegated) legislation is a term used to describe law made by ministers (or other bodies), with powers provided by an Act of Parliament.[2]

Statutory Instruments (SIs): SIs are the main form in which secondary legislation is introduced in the UK. An Act of Parliament provides the power to make a statutory instrument and is usually conferred on a Minister of the Crown, who can then introduce the relevant secondary legislation mentioned in the Act. SIs may follow affirmative or negative procedure, or have no procedure at all, but the Act stipulates which to use.[3]

Byelaws: Byelaws are laws made by a local council in accordance with power in a public general act or a local act which requires action in a particular area. These laws come with sanction or penalty if they are not complied with.[4]

Procedural Rules: Rules on procedure constitute a procedural code, the main aim of which is to ensure courts handle cases in the proper way.[5]

Orders in Council: Orders in Council are a regulation issued by the Crown on the advice of the Privy Council. However, in modern times, orders are only issued following advice from Ministers. The redistribution of functions between Ministers is an example, using powers provided by an Act of Parliament. Another type of order, used to make appointments to the civil

---

[1] Gillespie and Weare, pp. 25-27.

[2] UK Parliament, 'Delegated legislation', https://www.parliament.uk/site-information/glossary/delegated-or-secondary-legislation/ (accessed 1 February 2021).

[3] UK Parliament, 'Statutory instruments (SIs)', https://www.parliament.uk/site-information/glossary/statutory-instruments-sis/ (accessed 1 February 2021).

[4] 'Guidance: Local government legislation byelaws', https://www.gov.uk/guidance/local-government-legislation-byelaws#introduction (accessed 1 February 2021).

[5] Justice, 'Procedure rules', http://www.justice.gov.uk/courts/procedure-rules (accessed 1 February 2021).

service, is issued under the royal prerogative. While Orders in Council require approval by the monarch, the government drafts and controls them.[6]

5-) What are the advantages and disadvantages of using secondary legislation?

Advantages	Disadvantages
• Saves time; • Produced with specialist knowledge; • Control exercised by Parliament.	• Lack of oversight; • Lack of publicity; • Undemocratic; • Risk of sub-delegation.[7]

6-) What is the primary legislation-making process?

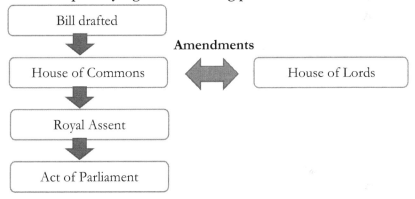

The legislative stages:[8]

First Reading: This is just a formal stage with no debate on the bill.

Second Reading: This entails a debate in the chamber on the main features of the bill. A government minister commences the debate by making a case for the bill and explaining the measures it contains. The opposition responds and members are then able to discuss it. The government then draws the debate to a conclusion by answering the points raised.

Committee Stage: At this stage the bill is subjected to a line-by-line evaluation. In the Commons a specially convened committee of MPs (a

---

[6] UK Parliament, 'Orders in council', https://www.parliament.uk/site-information/glossary/orders-in-council/ (accessed 1 February 2021).

[7] Thomas and McGourlay, p. 33.

[8] 'Guidance: Legislative process taking a bill through Parliament', https://www.gov.uk/guidance/legislative-process-taking-a-bill-through-parliament (accessed 1 February 2021).

Public Bill Committee), based on the balance of forces in the House, may carry out this evaluation.

Report Stage: At this stage, which takes place in the chamber in both Houses, if amendments have been tabled, they are discussed, if not, this is a purely formal stage. Just like in the committee stage, the amendments may alter what is in the bill, or lead to the addition of new provisions.

Third Reading: In the Commons this involves another general debate of the bill which usually happens straight after the Report stage (or, if the EVEL procedures apply, immediately after it has been examined by the Legislative Grand Committee as mentioned above). No amendments can be tabled. In the Lords, the Third Reading happens on a later day, and tidying up amendments may be tabled.

Later stages: Agreement on the text of a bill is required in both Houses in order for it to become an act. Therefore, if the bill is amended in the Lords, it must be sent back to the Commons for these amendments to be scrutinised. The first House can, if it wishes, reject the amendments, alter them or propose alternatives. Hence, it is quite possible for a bill to move between the two Houses several times before agreement is reached. As a result, this stage is often referred to as "ping pong".

Royal Assent: After a bill has been passed by both Houses it becomes law once it receives Royal Assent. The bill then becomes an act.

7-) What is the difference between white and green papers?

White Papers are Government documents that contain policy statements and set out future plans. White Papers are published as Command Papers and may incorporate proposals for future legislation. A White Paper paves the way for comment and debate with interested parties before changes that are made prior to a Bill being taken to Parliament.[9]

Green Papers are prepared by the Government for discussion of proposals that are still at a formative stage. Such discussions take place in Parliament and outside, in order to provide feedback to the department that prepares the Green Paper.[10]

---

[9] UK Parliament, 'White Papers', https://www.parliament.uk/site-information/glossary/white-paper/ (accessed 1 February 2021).
[10] UK Parliament, 'Green Papers', https://www.parliament.uk/site-information/glossary/green-papers/?id=32625 (accessed 1 February 2021).

8-) Who are the law-makers?

Branch of state	Description	Role
Legislature	Houses of Parliament, including the House of Commons and the House of Lords, and the Monarch.	The main role of the legislature is to make the law. It is the primary and supreme law-making body in the country.
Executive	It includes the Prime Minister, his/her cabinet members and civil servants.	The main role of the executive is to implement the law. But the executive also possesses broad law-making powers by means of the utilisation of secondary legislation, and it can also use prerogative powers to take action and create policy.
Judiciary	Courts, including senior and first-instance courts.	The main role of the judiciary is to interpret and apply the law. They also participate in law-making by developing common law.

9-) Who are the influencers on the law-makers?

The main examples of influencers on the law-makers are as follows:

The Law Commission is a statutory independent body established to review the law and make recommendations to ensure it continues to be fair, modern, simple and cost-effective. The Law Commission undertakes research and submits its recommendations to Parliament for consideration. It also has a responsibility to standardise law and ensure that outdated acts are repealed.[11]

The public, media and campaign (pressure) groups also wield influence over legislators. Campaign groups are formed by people who share opinions and wish to effect reform of laws. Examples of such groups are Amnesty International, Human Rights Watch, Greenpeace, Liberty and Fathers4justice. These groups carry out activities such as organising meetings and rallies, publicity campaigns, lobbying MPs and encouraging the public to sign petitions calling for legal reforms. They use the media to publicise their aims as a way to attain their objectives.

---

[11] Law Commission, 'About us', https://www.lawcom.gov.uk/about/ (accessed 1 February 2021).

10-) How should you read the legislation?

The legislation should be read as a whole by focusing on the following details **(intrinsic aids)** as follows:

1. Short Title
2. Citation
3. Long Title
4. Date of Royal Assent
5. Enacting formula
6. Sections
    i. Date of commencement
    ii. Any geographical limitations
    iii. Definition sections
7. Marginal Notes
8. Schedules

The **extrinsic aids** could also be used to interpret the legislation:

1. Dictionary;
2. Explanatory notes;
3. Presumptions;
4. Law commissioners' reports;
5. Judicial precedents;
6. Previous statutes;
7. Hansard;
8. HRA 1998;
9. Rules of interpretation.

In addition, it should be noted that if the statute is written thus: s7(2)(a)(i), it means Section 7; sub-section 2; paragraph a; sub-paragraph i.

11-) What are the rules of interpretation?

The Courts have the freedom to decide what is the most appropriate way to interpret the legislation. There are four different rules of interpretation:

Literal rule: The wording of a statute is interpreted in the most straightforward way possible. Judges just select the most evident, ordinary and natural meaning of a word (using a dictionary). It is not for judges to consider the result of the interpretation *(London and North Eastern Railway Co. v Berriman [1946] AC 278).*

Golden rule: In the event that the literal rule leads to absurdity, common sense should come into play. In other words, the judges work out what, in their opinion, was the intention of Parliament (***Stock v Frank Jones (Tipton) Ltd*** [1978] 1 All ER 948).

Mischief rule: This rule looks at the original objective of the provisions being assessed (***Heydon's Case*** (1584) 3 Co Rep 7a, 7b). The purpose is to interpret the rule in a way that fulfils its objective(s) – only examining the situation before the Act was introduced to work out what they consider parliament's intention was. The courts are obliged to take four issues into consideration:

1. Before the Act came into force what was the common law?
2. What was the inadequacy of the common law which did not sufficiently address the mischief or defect?
3. With what solution or remedy did Parliament intend to correct the defect in question?
4. Why did Parliament opt for that particular means of resolving the matter?

Purposive rule: This rule examines the social and economic context of the Act. The purposive rule of interpretation is broader than the mischief rule, although it originates from that rule (***R v Secretary of State for Health exp Quintavalle*** [2003] UKHL 13).

12-) Where can you find legislation?

- Online resources (eg: Lexis Nexus/Westlaw);
- www.legislation.gov.uk;
- Textbooks;
- Halsbury's statutes;
- Current Law series.

CASE STUDY:

Oakfield solicitors have asked you to advise Julie concerning whether she has any criminal liability under the Nudity Act 2020. Julie was arrested on Southend Beach after a complaint by Mrs Jackson. The complainant was on Southend Beach watching her daughter, who was playing volleyball, when Julie suddenly emerged from the sea totally naked. Mrs Jackson says that Julie went over to her towel and lay there in the sun. Mrs Jackson said she was 'horrified' as such incidents do not occur on Southend beach. She further claims that everyone was shocked by the sight of Julie and the volleyball match had to be abandoned.

By utilising the various methods of statutory interpretation and the words used, etc. advise Julie as to whether she has committed an offence under the Nudity Act 2020.

NUDITY ACT 2020 (fictitious)

This Act is to prevent members of the public from removing clothes in public areas.

Section 1

It shall be an offence to:

(1) disrupt sporting and cultural events by removing all clothing, when it should have been foreseen that this would cause disruption to the event; or

(2) remove all clothing in parks, shopping centres and picnic areas; or

(3) remove clothing to a state of semi-nudity in theatres, shops and other such places.

Is it a sporting and cultural event?

Focus should be on the use of AND rather than OR – **does an event have to be both? This narrows the field (may cover horse racing and tennis – but not volleyball)?**

The words need to be examined in the context of the Act itself and the courts scrutinising the Act in its entirety to ascertain whether a contentious word is more clearly defined in another place. The prosecution might make the case that the word 'events' implies either sporting or cultural, and it not necessarily having to be both.

So, is it a sporting event?

According to the *literal rule* based on the dictionary definition of the words in the statute, it could be argued that this is a sporting event. The external aid of a dictionary could be consulted to define the word.

Sporting event - what is an event? What is sporting? Are they amateurs? Is this the type of event intended?

The Cambridge English Dictionary defines sport as an activity needing physical effort and skill that is played according to rules, for enjoyment or as a job.

The word cultural refers to the habits, traditions and beliefs of a society, and to heritage and the arts.

An event is something that happens, particularly something that is important or unusual.[12]

Think about any way this could be challenged?

The defence might ask that other rules should be considered. In the event that the literal interpretation is ridiculous (not just unfair) the **golden rule** could be invoked, as it has a common-sense approach.

Alternatively, the **mischief rule**, as established in **Heydon's case,** could be invoked, as that looks at the objective of the Act and the situation of relevant common law prior to the introduction of the Act to identify the mischief which the Act was designed to prevent.

Another source is the **purposive rule**, which is broader than the mischief rule as it examines the social and economic implications of the Act in addition to the common law and the mischief targeted.

The external aid of Hansard might be consulted in the event of ambiguity, but it is important to remember that the contributions of backbenchers will be ignored: **Pepper (Inspector of Taxes) v Hart [1992] UKHL 3.** Only what is said by the proposer of the Act or the minister in question will be considered, in this case the Home Secretary's comments are relevant. What a backbencher said about beaches must be ignored.

Did she remove all her clothes?

- '....**by** removing all clothing, **when it should have been foreseen that this would cause disruption to the event.**'

The use of the word 'by' necessitates a causal link between the Act of undressing and the disruption of the event. The taking off of garments must have led to the disruption – a link that is apparent from the wording of the statute.

However, it is also possible to argue that the person taking off her clothes should have 'foreseen' disruption. The committing of an offence needs *mens rea* (thinking part; intention) unless it is categorically excluded **(Sweet v Parsley [1970] AC 132)**.

Is it the implication that this is a *mens rea*?

Yes, it is.

---

[12] Cambridge English Dictionary, https://dictionary.cambridge.org/dictionary/english/sport; https://dictionary.cambridge.org/dictionary/english/cultural; https://dictionary.cambridge.org/dictionary/english/event (accessed 1 February 2021).

Is the beach included within s1(2)?

Rules concerning language may be used. The Act specifically mentions parks, shopping centres and picnic areas. The incident in question took place on a beach. The principle: *Expressio Unius est Exclusio Alterius* (when one or more things of a class are expressly mentioned, others of the same class are excluded) may be invoked. Since other provisions contain words such as 'and other such places' whereas here there is a complete list, it may be inferred that the intention of Parliament was to only include those places that are mentioned.

It is possible to claim that a beach is a picnic area, but according to *Noscitur a sociis* (A court will examine words in the context of the Act in its entirety) the meaning of a word can be derived from its association with other words. A park could be considered as a picnic area, but there is a specific reference to parks in the Act.

CHAPTER III

SOURCE OF LAW II: CASE LAW

Learning Outcomes:

In this chapter, you should be able to understand:

- ✓ the doctrine of precedent in the common law system;
- ✓ the binding elements of a judgment;
- ✓ which cases and elements of a case are persuasive;
- ✓ where to find case law;
- ✓ the anatomy of a case.

Questions and Answers

1-) What is the doctrine of precedent in the common law system?

The doctrine of precedent is also known as *stare decisis*. It means that a court has an obligation to comply with a legal rule/principle when it has been determined by a higher court – one to which the court is linked. That is, judgments of higher courts are binding on lower courts:[1]

CIVIL LAW CASES:

Supreme Court	**BINDS**	Court of Appeal (Civil)	**BINDS**	High Court

CRIMINAL LAW CASES:

Supreme Court	**BINDS**	Court of Appeal (Criminal)	**BINDS**	Crown Courts & Magistrates Courts

---

[1] BPP, pp. 54-59.

2-) **What are the advantages and disadvantages of the doctrine of precedent?[2]**

Advantages	Disadvantages
• Certainty/predictability of the law. • Practicality. Lawyers may base their advice to clients on foreseeing the conclusion. • Flexibility in developing the law. Courts are still able to improve the law, for example, it may be out of date. • Adaptability to changing circumstances.	• Rigidity. There may not be as much certainty as thought on account of courts differentiating between cases, hence avoiding precedent. • The potential sacrifice of considerations of wider issues. • Often an unjust precedent can lead to future injustices. • A high volume of cases. • Slowness in adapting the law to practical reality.

3-) What are the forms of judgments?

Judgment	Meaning
Unanimous	All judges agreed on the verdict.
Majority	The court reached its decision in a majority agreement e.g. 2-1 in the Court of Appeal or 3-2 in the Supreme Court.
Dissenting	A minority judgment. Judge disagrees with the majority.

4-) What is the levels of the court structure?

There are two basic levels within the court structure:

(a) Senior Courts:

(i) The Supreme Court (and pre 1.10.2009, it was the House of Lords);
(ii) Court of Appeal (Civil/Criminal Divisions);
(iii) High Court;
(iv) Crown Court.

(b) Inferior Courts:

(i) Small claims court (though technically a procedure rather than a court);
(ii) County Courts;
(iii) Magistrates' Courts;
(iv) Youth Courts.

---

[2] Ibid., p. 58.

5-) What is the hierarchy of the court system?

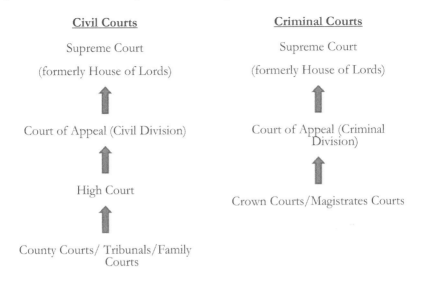

Civil Courts	Criminal Courts
Supreme Court (formerly House of Lords)	Supreme Court (formerly House of Lords)
Court of Appeal (Civil Division)	Court of Appeal (Criminal Division)
High Court	Crown Courts/Magistrates Courts
County Courts/ Tribunals/Family Courts	

6-) Who are the parties in the court system?

✓ **Civil Law**

The Claimant (previously the Plaintiff): The party bringing the case.

The Defendant: The party defending the case.

The Appellant: The party bringing the action in an appeal.

The Defendant or the Respondent: The party defending an appeal case.

✓ **Criminal Law**

The Prosecutor: The party bring criminal proceedings against a person.

The Defendant: The party defending the case.

7-) What is the role of the Judicial Committee of the Privy Council? How do its judgments affect domestic law?

The Judicial Committee of the Privy Council (JCPC) is the highest court of appeal for the UK overseas territories and Crown dependencies. It is also the highest court of appeal for Commonwealth countries that still have this final appeal, both those that maintain the appeal to Her Majesty in Council, and republics, that refer cases to the Judicial Committee.[3]

The JCPC consists of judges who also sit in the Supreme Court. Therefore, decisions of the Council are considered to carry weight. The JCPC's place as regards precedence was addressed by the Supreme Court in the **Willers case** *(Willers v Joyce and another (No 2) [2016] UKSC 44)*. The Court found that JCPC's decisions are merely persuasive. However, it did list the following exceptions:

(i) A practice direction exists according to which it is necessary for applicants to the JCPC to state that their appeal entails calling on the JCPC to depart from a decision of the Supreme Court. This procedure should also apply to the Court of Appeal.

(ii) The President of the JCPC is then able to consider this when deciding on the form and size of the panel which hears the case.

(iii) The court is then able to find that the Supreme Court or Court of Appeal judgment was incorrect, and, furthermore, direct national courts to consider the JCPC's decision binding.

8-) Are Courts bound by their previous judgments?

For the Supreme Court: In the past it was the case that the House of Lords was bound by its own jurisprudence. However, the Practice Statement of 1966 was published indicating that in certain conditions it could depart from its decisions. This document has been deemed to apply to the Supreme Court.

Previous judgments of **the Court of Appeal** are binding for the Court of Appeal Civil Division apart from three exceptions *(Young v Bristol Aeroplane Co [1944] KB 718)*:

(i) If there are conflicting Court of Appeal decisions, the court is free to select the decision to follow. Such cases may take place at the same or a similar time. In 1990 two different Courts of Appeal held hearings to determine the meaning of the word 'maliciously' in the Offences Against the Person Act of 1861 in rooms next to each other on the same day. It seems strange that the meaning of this word had not been determined previously, and even stranger that the two courts decided on two different definitions.

(ii) If the Supreme Court is considered to have overruled the judgment in question impliedly.

---

[3] 'Judicial Committee of the Privy Council', https://www.jcpc.uk/ (accessed 1 February 2021).

(iii) If the decision in question is *per incurium*. That is, if the decision is erroneous. This generally means that a case that should have been referenced has been overlooked.

For criminal division: Here things are not as rigorous. In **R v Taylor** it was ruled that flexibility is appropriate if a person's liberty is at stake *(R v Taylor [1950] 2 KB 368)*.

For High Court: Previous judgments are deemed persuasive, not binding.

9-) What is the anatomy of a case?

Civil cases

In most civil cases it looks like this: **Bolton v Stone**. It is pronounced Bolton and Stone rather than Bolton versus Stone.

Criminal cases

Criminal cases are generally set out in this way: **R v Hasan**. R stands for Rex or Regina. In spoken language it is: 'Crown against Hasan'.

Occasionally this formulation occurs: **CC of Avon and Somerset Police v Shimmen**

This formulation also used to be used: **Anderton v Ryan**. Prior to the introduction of the Crown Prosecution Service, more cases appeared like this.

The need for confidentiality

When confidentiality is deemed to be necessary, just an initial will suffice. In the case cited C is probably a minor. In civil cases a clue is usually given regarding the nature of the case. Re A (conjoined twins) is a significant case, but it would be much harder to locate if it was referred to as Re A. Since there are numerous cases listed as Re A the date would be needed to find it.

Judicial Review

Until 2001 they were listed as **R v Medical Appeal Tribunal ex parte Gilmore**. In this case, Gilmore applied for a review of a decision of the Medical Appeal Tribunal. Since 2001 cases are referred to as **R (on the application of CC of Greater Manchester Police v Salford Magistrates Court**. In this case the Chief Constable of Greater Manchester Police applied for a review of a Salford Magistrates Court judgment.

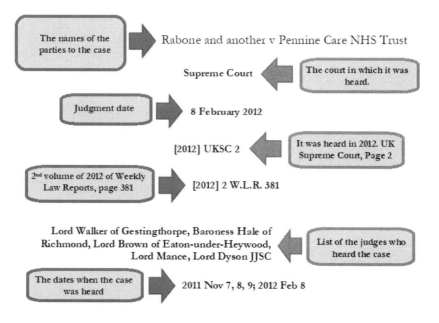

10-) Where can you find cases?

Judgments are published in law reports by independent organisations.

There is a hierarchy.

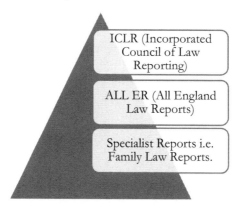

The Incorporated Council of Law Reporting reports are:

- AC (Appeal cases - Supreme Court/House of Lords)
- KBD/QBD (Kings/Queens Bench - Court of Appeal and the Queen's Bench Division of the High Court).
- Ch (Chancery - Court of Appeal and the Chancery Division of the High Court),

- WLR (Weekly Law Reports)

It should be noted that a large number of judgments are now available online:

- Supreme Court: www.supremecourt.gov.uk/decided-cases/index.html;
- British & Irish Legal Information Institute: www.bailii.org;
- Lawtel;
- LexisNexis;
- Westlaw.

CASE STUDY:

There are two professional boxers, Alex and Justine, who are fierce rivals. According to the rules of boxing 'Boxers must not punch an opponent after the bell signifying the end of a round' has rung.

During a match, Alex hits Justine in the face. As Justine aims to hit Alex back, the bell rings, but Justine cannot stop and punches Alex in the face, damaging his eye, leading to his losing all sight in that eye. The referee disqualifies Justine for an 'illegal, after the bell' blow and declares Alex the winner of the bout.

Justine was charged with causing grievous bodily harm to Alex under Section 20 of the Offences Against the Persons Act 1861. After Justine was convicted of the Section 20 offence in the Crown Court, he is now appealing against his conviction to the Court of Appeal.

After the decision in *R v Barnes*, explain whether you anticipate the Court of Appeal quashing or upholding Justine's conviction and why you foresee such a judgment.

Section 20: Inflicting bodily injury, with or without weapon.

Whosoever shall unlawfully and maliciously wound or inflict any grievous bodily harm upon any other person, either with or without any weapon or instrument, shall be guilty of a misdemeanour, and being convicted thereof shall be liable . . . F1 to be kept in penal servitude . . .

Suggested answer:

There are two fundamental elements of any criminal offence: *actus reas* and *mens rea*.

Firstly, these elements should be applied in Section 20 offence:

- Actus Reus:
  Wound OR Cause GBH

31

- Actus Reus:
  Intention OR Reckless as to causing some harm (at moment committing the AR)

Secondly, you should start by identifying the ratio of Barnes *(See the following link for R v Barnes, 2004] EWCA Crim 3246; [2005] 1 WLR 910: https://www.bailii.org/ew/cases/EWCA/Crim/2004/3246.html):*

Lord Woolf states the ratio in para. 12: 'If what occurs goes beyond what a player can reasonably be regarded as having accepted by taking part in the sport, this indicates that the conduct will not be covered by the defence.'

And in paras. 15 & 16:

- *Played within the rules of the game*
- *If outside rules & in highly competitive sport- just heat of the moment? depends (objective)*
- *Type of sport*
- *Level at which it is played*
- *Nature of the act*
- *Degree of force used*
- *The extent of risk of injury*
- *State of mind of the defendant*
- *Was the contact so obviously late and/or violent so not:*
  - *an instinctive reaction*
  - *Error or misjudgment in the heat of the game*

Application part: The legal principle should be applied to the given facts.

Because Justine's punch was thrown after the bell and was therefore outside the rules of boxing, does not necessarily mean that he cannot raise the defence of consent; the question is whether this kind of punch is 'reasonably acceptable' as part of boxing.

Work through the criteria (paras. 15 &16 – Lord Woolf (Barnes)).

Applying this criteria – you can conclude either this is or is not reasonably acceptable.

EG - arguably, since Justine was throwing the punch just as the bell sounded, this was just an error of judgement and therefore within what is reasonably acceptable for this sport.

Would your reply be different if, at the end of the round when both boxers were in their respective corners, Justine had dashed across the ring in fury and punched Alex in the face?

Yes – such a response would not be considered acceptable in boxing.

Would your answer in the question above be different if Alex had died as a consequence of Justine's last punch, rather than only suffering an eye injury?

No – the degree of the resulting injury has no effect on the applicability of the ratio mentioned by Lord Woolf.

CHAPTER IV

SOURCE OF LAW III: INTERNATIONAL LAW

Learning Outcomes:

In this chapter, you should be able to understand:

- ✓ the key sources of international law;
- ✓ how European Union (EU) law has had an impact on domestic law;
- ✓ how European Court of Human Rights' case law has had an impact upon domestic law;
- ✓ how international law affects domestic law.

Questions and Answers:

1-) Is the UK a monist or dualist state?

The UK is a dualist state, meaning that international treaties only have effect in domestic law when they are made part of domestic legislation. For example, EU Treaties were introduced to domestic law by the ECA 1972. Similarly, the ECHR was made part of domestic law by the HRA 1998.

Almost all European legal systems are monist. This system involves considering all branches of law as being part of a single, binding legal system. If there is any clash between domestic and international law, the international law rule is superior and overrides the domestic rule.

2-) What are the prominent international institutions of which the UK is a part?

Currently, the UK is still a part of the Council of Europe (CoE) and the United Nations (UN). In addition, the UK was a part of the EU between 1 January 1973 and 31 January 2020.

3-) What is the EU?

The EU is a group of 27 countries in Europe. All 27 countries work together to make sure that:

- ✓ there is peace in Europe;

✓ people have good lives;
✓ things are fair for all people and nobody is left out;
✓ the languages and cultures of all people are respected;
✓ there is a strong European economy and countries use the same coin to do business together.[1]

4-) What are the institutions of the EU and their functions?

Council of the European Union: Composed of ministers from the Member States. Its functions are as follows: to represent the Member States' governments; to make legislation with the European Parliament; to make and coordinate policies; to sign international treaties; to deal with the scrutiny and approval of the budget with the European Parliament; to develop the EU's common foreign and security policy.

Court of Justice: It is located in Luxembourg. Its functions are as follows: to interpret and enforce EU law; to determine the validity of EU acts and legislation; to make rulings on preliminary references from national courts.

European Central Bank: Its functions are as follows: to be responsible for conducting the monetary policy of these Member States; to comprise Member States which have the Euro as their currency; to maintain price stability in the EU; to co-operate with the central banks of all Member States.

European Commission: Composed of one Commissioner from each Member State; President of the Commission; High Representative of the Union for Foreign Affairs and Security Policy. Its functions are as follows: to initiate legislation; to administer policies and programmes; to draft the annual EU budget; to manage the budget and allocate funding; to enforce EU Law; to negotiate international treaties; to represent the EU on certain international bodies.

European Council: Composed of Heads of State or Government of the Member States; President of the European Council and President of the European Commission. Its functions are as follows: to provide the necessary impetus for the EU's development; to define the general political directions and priorities thereof; to deal with complex and politically sensitive issues.

European Court of Auditors: Its function is as follows: to audit the revenue and expenditure of the EU.

---

[1] The European Union, 'About the EU', https://europa.eu/european-union/about-eu/easy-to-read_en (accessed 1 February 2021).

European Parliament: Composed of 705 members (MEPs) elected by the citizens of the Member States for five-year terms. It is located in Strasbourg, but the Committees of the Parliament sit in Brussels. Its functions are as follows: to make law; to scrutinise and approve the EU budget; to supervise other institutions such as the European Commission; to debate issues related to the EU.

5-) What are the legal sources of EU Law? Are they legally binding on member states?

Primary: Treaties.

Secondary: Regulations; Directives and Decisions.

Case Law: Judgments of the EU Courts.

Soft-Law: Recommendations; Opinions and others.

Treaty is a primary legal source in EU Law. It consists of the Treaty on the Functioning of the European Union (TFEU) and the Treaty on the European Union (TEU). They are legally binding on member states.

Regulation is a secondary legal source in EU Law. Regulations are enforceable in all Member States, coming into effect immediately without the need for any measures by these states. They are also binding on member states (Article 288 TFEU).

Directives are a secondary binding legal source in EU Law. According to Article 288 of the TFEU, directives are addressed to Member States which have to implement them. Member states have the obligation to implement directives within the stated deadline in the directive. In the event the directive has no deadline, then they must be introduced within 20 days of the publication of the directive (Article 297 TFEU).

A decision addressed to particular recipients shall only be binding on them. It shall be binding in its entirety (Article 288 TFEU).

Case-law is the judgments of the EU Courts (The Court of Justice and the European Court of Auditors). Their judgments have binding force.

Soft-Law mainly are recommendations and opinions. According to Article 288 TFEU, they are not legally binding. Other forms of soft-law are: Communications, Declarations, Notices, Programmers and Resolutions.

With regards to the impact of the above-mentioned EU law sources into the UK domestic law, the ECA 1972 was an important piece of legislation.

Section 2(1) of the ECA 1972 provided that:

All such rights, power, liabilities, obligations and restrictions from time to time created or arising by or under the Treaties, and all such remedies and procedures from time to time provided for, by or under the Treaties, as in accordance with the Treaties are without further enactment to be given legal effect or used in the United Kingdom shall be recognised and available in law, and be enforced, allowed and followed accordingly, and the expression 'enforceable Community right' … shall be read as referring to one which this subjection applies.

Section 3 stipulated that all issues regarding the meaning and effect of EU law should be ascertained according to the principles established by the relevant court of the EU. The most important aspect of this law was that section 2(4) of the Act stressed that all British legislation, including future laws, was to be interpreted and applied in line with EU law. Consequently, British courts were to no longer base judgments on provisions which did not comply with EU law. This was eventually confirmed by the House of Lords in *R v Secretary of State for Transport, ex parte Factortame (No.2) [1991] 1 AC 603.*

6-) What is the Council of Europe (CoE)?

The CoE was founded in 1949. It is one of the largest and oldest European organisations, with 47 member states. It advocates and seeks to protect the fundamental aspects of Human Rights. Its aims are as follows:

- To protect human rights, pluralist democracy and the rule of law;
- To promote awareness and encourage the development of Europe's cultural identity and diversity;

- To seek solutions to problems facing European society, such as: discrimination against minorities, xenophobia, intolerance, environmental protection, human cloning, terrorism, human trafficking, organised crime and corruption, cybercrime, violence against children;

- To help consolidate democratic stability in Europe by backing political, legislative and constitutional reform.[2]

7-) What are the Institutions of the CoE and their functions?

Commissioner for Human Rights: This is an independent and impartial body in the CoE. The Commissioner encourages education and the importance of human rights in the member states of the CoE. The Commissioner also visits member states, looking to overcome problems in

---

[2] Council of Europe, 'Objectives and mission', https://www.coe.int/en/web/sarajevo/objectives-mission (accessed 1 February 2021).

the safeguarding of human rights and promoting reform. The Commissioner attaches particular importance to the rights of children in all his activities.

Committee of Ministers: The CoE's decision-making institution. The Committee of Ministers consists of the foreign affairs ministers of the member states or their permanent diplomatic representatives in Strasbourg. The Committee of Ministers has issued recommendations to member states on various issues, including the rights of children.

Committee on Social Affairs, Health and Sustainable Development: This Committee deals with questions relating to children's rights.

Conference of International Non-governmental Organisations (Conference of INGOs): This body represents the views of civil society at the CoE. Non-governmental organisations can participate in the decision-making processes of the CoE by means of the Conference of INGOs. INGOs also have the right to gain participatory status at the CoE, engage in consultation and become actively involved in specific projects.

Congress of Local and Regional Authorities: This is a political assembly consisting of 636 members that have been voted into office in local and regional authorities in the 47 member states of the CoE. The Congress has played a key role in the CoE's efforts to prevent sexual violence against children.

European Court of Human Rights (ECtHR): It is located in Strasbourg. The Court deals with applications by individuals or states regarding violations of the rights enshrined in the ECHR, which has been ratified by all 47 CoE member states. Citizens of these states consequently have the right to apply to the Court.

Parliamentary Assembly: The Assembly enables 318 representatives from parliaments in the CoE to debate significant questions of human rights and criticise the human rights records of member states.[3]

8-) What is the European Convention on Human Rights (ECHR)?

The ECHR, also known as the Convention for the Protection of Human Rights and Fundamental Freedoms, was adopted in 1950 and entered into force in 1953. The Convention was the first document to enshrine a number of the rights contained in the Universal Declaration of Human Rights and

---

[3] Council of Europe, 'CoE Institutions', https://www.coe.int/en/web/children/coe-institutions (accessed 1 February 2021).

make them binding. In other words, this Convention was designed to protect human rights, democracy and the rule of law.

The Convention has been updated and more rights have been added to the original text since 1950. At present there are 15 additional protocols.

9-) What does the ECHR contain?

The following rights, in particular, are protected:

- ✓ Right to life (Article 2);
- ✓ Prohibition of torture (Article 3);
- ✓ Prohibition of slavery and forced labour (Article 4);
- ✓ Right to liberty and security (Article 5);
- ✓ Right to a fair trial (Article 6);
- ✓ No punishment without law (Article 7);
- ✓ Right to respect for private and family life (Article 8);
- ✓ Freedom of thought, conscience and religion (Article 9);
- ✓ Freedom of expression (Article 10);
- ✓ Freedom of assembly and association (Article 11);
- ✓ Right to marry (Article 12);
- ✓ Right to an effective remedy (Article 13);
- ✓ Prohibition of discrimination (Article 14)
- ✓ Protection of property (Additional protocol 1, Article 1);
- ✓ Right to education (Additional protocol 1, Article 2);
- ✓ Right to free elections (Additional protocol 1, Article 3).

Please note that there is no explicit hierarchy of rights in the Convention.

10-) What are the categories of the ECHR rights?

1) **Absolute rights:** Rights that are non-derogable, meaning the state cannot place limitations on them: articles 3, 4 and 7.
2) **Limited rights:** The state can, in some circumstances, legitimately place limits on these rights: articles 2, 5 and 6. The exceptions to this rule are mentioned in the articles in question (termed 'limitations').

3) **Qualified rights:** Articles 8, 9, 10 and 11 are deemed qualified rights. The first paragraph of these articles outlines the right(s) to be protected by the Convention. In the second paragraph these rights are then qualified with information given as to how the state may lawfully impose restrictions.[4]

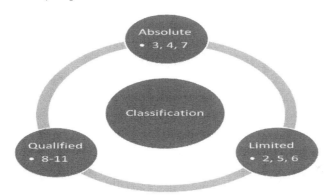

11-) What does the European Court of Human Rights (ECtHR) do?

The Court implements the ECHR. It has a responsibility to safeguard the rights and guarantees enshrined in the Convention and to ensure compliance by member States. The Court employs two fundamental principles, the 'margin of appreciation' and 'proportionality' to delineate the boundaries of state liability and individual rights.

It accepts complaints (called "applications") made by individuals or, occasionally, by States. When the Court finds that a member State has contravened one or more of these rights, the Court hands down a judgment documenting a violation.[5]

12-) Are the ECtHR's judgments legally binding on member states?

Firstly, according to Article 1 of the ECHR, "The High Contracting Parties shall secure to everyone within their jurisdiction the rights and freedoms defined in Section I of this Convention."

Secondly, according to Article 46(1) of the ECHR, "The High Contracting Parties undertake to abide by the final judgment of the Court in any case to which they are parties."

---

[4] Harris and others, pp. 108-109.
[5] 'European Court of Human Rights', https://echr.coe.int/Pages/home.aspx?p=home (accessed 1 February 2021).

In sum, the countries concerned are under an obligation to comply with the judgments of the ECtHR. However, the UK introduced HRA 1998 stating clearly in Section 2(1) that UK courts must take ECtHR's case law 'into account' when dealing with issues linked to a right enshrined in the ECHR. It is worthy of note that before the enactment of the HRA in 1998, people in England and Wales wishing to benefit from rights enshrined in the Convention had to go to the ECtHR. Presently, once a victim exhausts all domestic remedies, s/he can still go to the ECtHR.

The first judgment that considered the meaning and scope of HRA 1998, Section 2(1) was *R (Alconbury Developments Ltd) v Secretary of State for the Environment, [2001] UKHL 23*, a case in which the House of Lords found that, although ECtHR jurisprudence is not binding, national courts have an obligation to follow any appropriate case law unless there are particular circumstances, or ECtHR judgments leading to an outcome that fundamentally contradicts the apportioning of powers according to the UK constitution.

In *R (Ullah) v Special Adjudicator [2004] UKHL 26*, Lord Bingham made the observations set forth below, with which his fellow judges on the panel concurred:

> [T]he House is required by section 2(1) of the Human Rights Act 1998 to take into account any relevant Strasbourg case law. While such case law is not strictly binding, it has been held that courts should, in the absence of some special circumstances, follow any clear and constant jurisprudence of the Strasbourg court: R (Alconbury Developments Ltd) v Secretary of State for the Environment…, paragraph 26. This reflects the fact that the Convention is an international instrument, the correct interpretation of which can be authoritatively expounded only by the Strasbourg court. From this it follows that a national court subject to a duty such as that imposed by section 2 should not without strong reason dilute or weaken the effect of the Strasbourg case law … It is of course open to member states to provide for rights more generous than those guaranteed by the Convention, but such provision should not be the product of interpretation of the Convention by national courts, since the meaning of the Convention should be uniform throughout the states party to it. The duty of national courts is to keep pace with the Strasbourg jurisprudence as it evolves over time: no more, but certainly no less. (para. 20)

It is also worth noting that Section 3(1) stipulates that courts should interpret statutes thus: '… so far as it is possible to do so, primary legislation and subordinate legislation must be read and given effect in a way which is compatible with convention rights.'

Furthermore, courts are within their rights to state that a piece of primary legislation does not comply with the HRA 1998 (Section 4). That means, courts have the power to make a declaration of incompatibility.

13-) What is the United Nations (UN)?

The UN is an international body that was established in 1945. It at present consists of 193 Member States. The objectives and activities of the UN are based on the principles enshrined in its founding Charter.[6]

14-) What are the institutions of the UN and their functions?

There are six principal organs of the UN:

Economic and Social Council: The Economic and Social Council is a fundamental part of the UN system aiming for sustainable economic, social and environmental development. It plays a key role in encouraging debate and new ways of thinking, seeking agreement on ways to make progress, and coordinates endeavours to achieve objectives that have been agreed at an international level. It also undertakes development work after major UN conferences and summits.[7]

General Assembly: It has the power to make recommendations to States on international matters provided for in the UN Charter. It has also implemented actions of a political, economic, humanitarian, social and legal nature that have improved the lives of millions of people all over the world.[8]

International Court of Justice: It is the main judicial mechanism of the UN. It was founded in June 1945 by the Charter of the UN and held its first sitting in April 1946.[9]

Secretariat: The Secretariat has several departments, each of which has its own specific responsibilities. These offices and departments work in harmony so that the day to day global work of the UN is carried on smoothly in offices all over the world. The UN Secretary-General is the head of the UN Secretariat.[10]

---

[6] United Nations, 'About the UN', https://www.un.org/en/about-un/ (accessed 1 February 2021).

[7] United Nations Economic and Social Council, 'About Us', https://www.un.org/ecosoc/en/about-us (accessed 1 February 2021).

[8] General Assembly of the United Nations, 'Functions and powers of the General Assembly', https://www.un.org/en/ga/about/background.shtml (accessed 1 February 2021).

[9] International Court of Justice, 'The Court', https://www.icj-cij.org/en/court (accessed 1 February 2021).

[10] United Nations, 'Secretariat', https://www.un.org/en/sections/about-un/secretariat/ (accessed 1 February 2021).

Security Council: The Security Council's main responsibility is to ensure international peace and security. It consists of 15 Members, each having one vote. According to the UN Charter, all Member States must comply with decisions of the Security Council.[11]

Trusteeship Council: This council was established to monitor reports from the Administering Authority concerning the situation of the inhabitants of Trust Territories, and their political, economic, social and educational development. It is also tasked with dealing with petitions from these territories in conjunction with the Administering Authority, and engaging in special missions to Trust Territories. The Trusteeship Council comprises the five permanent members of the Security Council - China, France, the Russian Federation, the United Kingdom and the United States.[12]

Please note that the UN also encompasses 15 agencies and several programmes and bodies.

15-) Are the International Court of Justice's judgments binding?

Yes, they are binding on the states concerned. According to Article 94 UN Charter, "each Member of the United Nations undertakes to comply with the decision of [the Court] in any case to which it is a party."

PRACTICE:

1. Case:

Andrew has been the victim of wrongful arrest at the hands of a police officer. He is not inclined to make a fuss about it, as he does not think it is worth it and might make things worse. However, his brother, James, is very upset about it and is determined to take action against the local police force under the HRA 1998 in order to gain redress for his brother.

Is it possible for James to do this?

- **Section 7(1) of the HRA 1998**: "a person who claims that a public authority has acted in a way which is made unlawful [by section 6(1)] may …bring proceedings … but only if he is a victim of an unlawful act…"

---

[11] United Nations, 'United Nations Security Council', https://www.un.org/securitycouncil/ (accessed 1 February 2021).
[12] United Nations, 'Trusteeship Council', https://www.un.org/en/sections/about-un/trusteeship-council/ (accessed 1 February 2021).

- **Section 7(7) of the HRA 1998:** "For the purposes of this section, a person is a victim of an unlawful act only if he would be a victim for the purposes of Article 34 of the Convention if proceedings were brought in the European Court of Human Rights in respect of that act."

- **Article 34 of the ECHR:** "The Court may receive applications from any person, nongovernmental organisation or group of individuals claiming to be the victim of a violation by one of the High Contracting Parties of the rights set forth in the Convention or the Protocols thereto…"

In ***Klass v Germany*** a victim is described as a person who has been directly affected by the violation of a Convention right ***(Klass v Germany Application no. App no 5029/71, 6 September 1978)***.

Therefore, it is evident that James will be unable to lodge a HRA claim for Andrew as he was not directly affected.

2. Case:

Vladimir, a Russian national resident in England, had a similar experience.

Would it be possible for him to make a HRA claim? If so, is there a time limit for making a claim of this kind in court?

Regarding the protection of rights, nationality is not relevant.

Article 1 of the ECHR states: "The High Contracting Parties shall secure to everyone within their jurisdiction the rights and freedoms defined in Section I of this Convention."

Hence, a citizen of any country may lodge a claim under the HRA 1998 if they believe a public authority has breached a right safeguarded by the Convention.

Vladimir would thus have a year to lodge a claim, according to Section 7(5) of the HRA 1998.

3. Case:

James was a British soldier who suffered a fatal injury caused by a roadside bomb in Helmand Province in Afghanistan. It subsequently emerged that his wounds were made worse by a faulty protective helmet.

Could James's parents lodge a HRA 1998 claim in connection with this incident?

In this case there is a question of the scope of jurisdiction of the HRA 1998. Generally, jurisdiction concerns the territory of the state in question, as per Article 1 of the ECHR.

However, HRA 1998 can have extra-territorial application. In *Al-Skeini and others v the UK* the ECtHR broadened the scope of Convention law to cover Iraq, something the House of Lords (currently Supreme Court) had not done in the domestic case (in 2007). The ECtHR took the view that the British military authorities in that part of southern Iraq were responsible for security in the region. Hence, deaths caused by British soldiers there could be deemed to be within jurisdiction (not only the deaths, like Baha Mousa's, which resulted in British military bases) *(Al-Skeini and Others v the UK, Application no. 55721/07, 7 July 2011)*.

James's parents would thus, as his next of kin, have the right to make a claim under the HRA.

4. Case:

Section 6(1) of the HRA mentions the obligation for "public authorities" to act in a manner that is compatible with Convention rights.

Which of the following bodies would be considered core public authorities?

  (i)   **The Home Office.**
  (ii)   **The police**
  (iii) **Sainsbury's**
  (iv)   **Liverpool City Council**

There are two types of 'public authority': a) **'core'** public authorities, bodies which on account of their function are clearly public authorities, and b) **'hybrid'** public authorities, concerns like privatised utility companies, that do not seem to meet the criteria of a public authority, but carry out public functions.

This distinction between the two types of authority is significant as it seems that while 'core' public authorities have to meet the Section 6(1) obligation regarding all their functions, a 'hybrid' public authority only has this obligation as regards acts which are of a public character.

It is obvious that i), ii) and iv) are all core PAs, with an obligation under Section 6(1) for all their acts. They are public authorities that carry out core functions as an adjunct of the state.

CHAPTER V

THE CIVIL JUSTICE SYSTEM

Learning Outcomes:

In this chapter, you should be able to understand:

- ✓ the functions of the courts in the civil justice system;
- ✓ the fundamental features of civil litigation;
- ✓ the main tenets followed by the civil courts;
- ✓ the different kinds of process in civil litigation.

Questions and Answers:

1-) What does the civil justice system involve?

It involves private matters between private legal parties including individuals and companies. For example, in a case of tort or breach of contract a defendant may have to pay damages to the injured party, or have to abide by the conditions of an injunction.

Moreover, civil law also addresses some questions of public law. For instance, issues concerning the adoption and fostering of children are also public law matters.[1]

2-) What regulates the civil justice system?

Civil Procedure Rules (CPR) 1998 is a procedural code whose overriding aim is to provide civil procedure as well as to enable the civil courts (Court of Appeal - Civil Division; High Court of Justice and County Court) to deal with cases justly.[2] They replaced the Rules of the Supreme Court 1965 and the County Court Rules 1981.[3]

---

[1] Thomas and McGourlay, p. 198.
[2] The Civil Procedure Rules 1998, https://www.legislation.gov.uk/uksi/1998/3132/contents (accessed 1 February 2021).
[3] Ministry of Justice, 'Procedure Rules', https://www.justice.gov.uk/courts/procedure-rules (accessed 1 February 2021).

3-) What is the court hierarchy in the civil justice system? What are their functions?

<u>**Civil Courts**</u>

Supreme Court (formerly House of Lords)

Court of Appeal (Civil Division)

High Court

County Courts/Tribunals/Family Courts

Supreme Court: It is the ultimate appeal court for the entire UK and also hears civil cases. It considers appeals on legal principles that are of significance to the general public; focuses on important cases of a constitutional nature and continues to develop its role as the UK Supreme Court, being considered a forerunner in the common law world.[4]

Court of Appeal (Civil Division): It is one of two divisions of the Court of Appeal of England and Wales. It hears appeals against certain decisions by:

- all three divisions of the High Court of Justice and their specialist courts, including the Administrative Court;
- county courts;
- the Family Court.

It also hears appeals against certain decisions by the:

- Competition Appeal Tribunal
- Employment Appeal Tribunal
- Upper Tribunal (Administrative Appeals Chamber)
- Upper Tribunal (Immigration and Asylum Chamber)
- Upper Tribunal (Lands Chamber)
- Upper Tribunal (Tax and Chancery Chamber)[5]

---

[4] The Supreme Court, 'Role of The Supreme Court', https://www.supremecourt.uk/about/role-of-the-supreme-court.html (accessed 1 February 2021).
[5] 'Court of Appeal Civil Division', https://www.gov.uk/courts-tribunals/court-of-appeal-civil-division (accessed 1 February 2021).

High Court: Please see the following table for the structure of the High Court[6]:

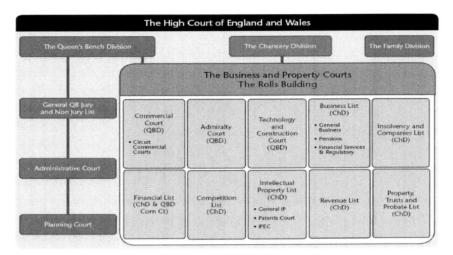

County Court: Three types of judges sit in the County Court: Circuit, Recorders and District Judges. The kinds of civil case heard in County Courts include:

- Businesses owed money endeavouring to recover outstanding debts;
- People who apply for compensation for injuries;
- Cases involving contract and tort (civil wrong) and cases lodged for recovery of land;
- Matters relating to bankruptcy and insolvency, also cases concerning wills and trusts (equity and contested probate actions) when the monetary value of the trust, fund or estate in question is of a sum up to £30,000;
- Landowners applying for orders to counter trespass.

It is worth noting that circuit judges usually deal with cases involving a value of more than £15,000 or of those that are important or complex.[7] Claims of less than £15,000 (or £1,000 in personal injury cases) automatically go to arbitration in front of a District Judge unless, for example, a complex

---

[6] Courts and Tribunals Judiciary, 'High Court', https://www.judiciary.uk/you-and-the-judiciary/going-to-court/high-court/ (accessed 1 February 2021).

[7] Courts and Tribunals Judiciary, 'County Court', https://www.judiciary.uk/you-and-the-judiciary/going-to-court/county-court/ (accessed 1 February 2021).

judicial question is at stake (Crime and Courts Act 2013).[8] If there is a particularly complex issue of law involved or a high sum of compensation requested, cases are usually referred to the High Court. Some areas of law (such as mortgages or bankruptcy) may have specific statutory provisions that determine which court has jurisdiction in matters, the county court or High Court.[9]

The Family Court: Family matters used to be heard either in Magistrates' Courts or the County Court, before a single Family Court was established by Section 17 Crime and Courts Act 2013, based on Section 31A of the Matrimonial and Proceedings Act 1984. This new court, that has been functioning since 22 April 2014, has jurisdiction in all family matters. The Family Court deals with the following issues:

- disagreements between parents over the raising of children;
- child protection initiatives taken by local authorities;
- divorce orders;
- financial backing for children following divorce or separation;
- certain matters relating to domestic violence;
- adoption.[10]

4-) Who are the parties in the civil justice system?

The Claimant (previously the Plaintiff): The party bringing the case.

The Defendant: The party defending the case.

The Appellant: The party bringing the action in an appeal.

The Defendant or the Respondent: The party defending an appeal case.

5-) What is the process of the civil justice system?

Civil justice cases are generally heard in county courts, although cases that are more serious or complicated are heard in the High Court. These cases range from relatively small or simple claims, for instance cases concerning merchandise that is damaged or debt recovery, to claims involving large sums of money lodged by large companies.

---

[8] HM Courts & Tribunals Service, 'The Fast Track and the Multi-Track in the civil courts', https://www.citizensadvice.org.uk/Global/Migrated_Documents/advisernet/04080403-ew-the-fast-track-and-the-multi-track-in-the-civil-courts-pdf-8.pdf (accessed 1 February 2021).
[9] BPP, p. 31.
[10] Courts and Tribunals Judiciary, 'Family Law Courts', https://www.judiciary.uk/you-and-the-judiciary/going-to-court/family-law-courts/ (accessed 1 February 2021).

Some civil cases take place in open court, which the public is free to attend, whereas other cases are heard and decided by the judge alone, based on the documents submitted.

Many civil disputes are resolved through recognised complaints procedures or alternative dispute resolution (ADR) and do not need to go court. Even when a case does go to court, the objective is to ensure the case is as straightforward as possible. For claims involving small sums of money the small claims court exists to provide a swift and inexpensive resolution of disputes.

Judges in civil courts cannot sentence a losing party to imprisonment. Generally, monetary damages are awarded to the successful party, the amount of which depends on the substance of the claim.[11]

Rule 26.1(2) of the CPR 1998 sets down these three tracks:

Small Claims Track: Claims of up to £10,000. An informal hearing in front of a district judge (County Court).

Fast Track: Claims of between £10,000 and £25,000, which are completed in one day. Requiring only one expert for each party.

Multi-track: Claims over £25,000 and those under £25,000 which need more than one day or more than one expert for each party.[12]

6-) What is the trial process in the civil justice system?

Prior to hearing the case, the judge studies the case papers in order to understand the details.

Most civil cases heard in court are without a jury (main exceptions being libel and slander cases). The judge reaches a decision after establishing the facts and applying the appropriate law - there may be disputes as to what that law provides – and then hands down a reasoned judgment.

Judges also manage civil cases after they have commenced, ensuring they are heard in an efficient and smooth manner.

This entails:

- seeking the co-operation of parties in the case to ensure a smooth process;
- assisting the parties to reach settlement of the case;

---

[11] Courts and Tribunals Judiciary, 'Civil Justice in England and Wales', https://www.judiciary.uk/about-the-judiciary/the-justice-system/jurisdictions/civil-jurisdiction/ (accessed 1 February 2021).
[12] Thomas and McGourlay, p. 213.

- if appropriate, directing the parties to an alternative dispute resolution procedure; and
- monitoring developments in a case.

In some cases, the parties will concur regarding facts and, consequently, the judge will not need to hear any evidence. There may be questions regarding the law to be applied or the judgment to be handed down. But generally, written and live evidence will be presented by the parties and their witnesses and witnesses may be cross-examined in court. The judge has an obligation to make sure that all parties are able to explain their case and have it considered in full. The judge may ask questions at any time in order to clarify relevant points. The judge is also responsible for procedural matters that may be raised during a hearing.

Judgment

After all the evidence from all parties involved and any submissions (representations) have been heard, the judge delivers judgment. This may be immediately after the hearing, or in complex cases, at a later date.

Civil judges are able to impose punishment on parties if, for instance, they are in contempt of court but, as a rule, civil cases do not result in any punishment being imposed.

In the event that the judge concludes that the claimant has the right to damages, he or she will decide what sum to award. Or perhaps the claimant has applied for an injunction – for instance, to ban the defendant from playing drums in an upstairs flat upstairs late at night, thus causing excessive noise - or a declaration – that is, an order pinpointing the exact boundary between two properties over which there has been a long disagreement. It is up to the judge to decide what the appropriate remedy is, if a remedy exists, and on the exact provisions of it.

7-) What do costs in the civil justice system involve?

After judgment in a case has been handed down, the judge must address the issue of the cost of the case. This may include lawyers' fees, court fees paid by the parties, fees charged by expert witnesses, allowances of litigants who have acted in person (without lawyers), lost earnings and travelling and other expenses of the parties and their witnesses. It is a general rule that the unsuccessful party pays the successful party's costs, but the judge has broad discretion as regards this rule. The judge's decision in this aspect of the case is very important for both parties. The judge may decide that the losing party is only liable to meet a part of the winning party's costs or that each party must meet their own costs. The judge is able to hear representations regarding costs at the conclusion of the case.[13]

8-) Is there any legal aid in the civil justice system? Is there any alternative way to access civil justice system?

The ECtHR found a violation of Article 6 of the ECHR in the case of **Steel and Morris v the UK** because the denial of legal aid to the applicants deprived them of the opportunity to present their case effectively before the court and contributed to an unacceptable inequality of arms **(Steel and Morris v the UK, Application no 68416/01, 15 February 2005, para. 72)**.

Indeed, legal aid is an important source to access civil justice (See Legal Aid, Sentencing and Punishment of Offenders Act -LASPO- 2012). Civil cases cover issues such as debt and problems concerning family or housing. To obtain legal aid, an individual generally has to prove they cannot afford meet legal costs by providing details and evidence of income, benefits, savings and property, including that of their partner. The issue in question also must be serious. If the applicant is under 18, they may have to provide information regarding the income of their parents or guardians.[14]

The Legal Aid Agency is an executive agency of the Ministry of Justice which deals with civil legal aid in England and Wales. The Agency's objectives are as follows:

- ✓ Provide simple, timely and reliable access to legal aid;
- ✓ Build strong relationships across Government and the justice system;
- ✓ Secure value for money for the taxpayer in all that we do;
- ✓ Achieve our full potential through being fair, proud and supportive.[15]

Legal aid is available for civil proceedings (Section 8 LASPO 2012):

(1) In this Part "legal services" means the following types of services—

(a) providing advice as to how the law applies in particular circumstances,

(b) providing advice and assistance in relation to legal proceedings,

---

[13] Courts and Tribunals Judiciary, https://www.judiciary.uk/about-the-judiciary/the-justice-system/jurisdictions/civil-jurisdiction/ (accessed 1 February 2021).

[14] 'Legal Aid', https://www.gov.uk/legal-aid/eligibility (accessed 1 February 2021).

[15] Legal Aid Agency, 'Annual Report and Accounts 2019-20', https://assets.publishing.service.gov.uk/government/uploads/system/uploads/attachment_data/file/902746/Legal_Aid_Agency_annual_report_and_accounts_2019_to_2020.pdf (accessed 1 February 2021).

(c) providing other advice and assistance in relation to the prevention of disputes about legal rights or duties ("legal disputes") or the settlement or other resolution of legal disputes, and

(d) providing advice and assistance in relation to the enforcement of decisions in legal proceedings or other decisions by which legal disputes are resolved.

(2) The services described in subsection (1) include, in particular, advice and assistance in the form of -

(a) representation, and

(b) mediation and other forms of dispute resolution.

(3) In this Part "civil legal services" means any legal services other than the types of advice, assistance and representation that are required to be made available under sections 13, 15 and 16 (criminal legal aid).

In addition, there are other alternative sources, such as Citizen Advice Bureaus, law centres and pro bono which can be used to gain access to civil justice. Or, alternatively, you can use your own resources such as insurance funding, conditional fee agreements and damage-based agreements to access justice.

Please note that there are two kinds of insurance funding: before the event insurance refers to the usual car or home insurance, whereas after the event insurance is usually taken out by claimants to cover the risk of costs. In addition, there are conditional fee agreements, usually called 'no win, no fee' agreements. Damages-based agreements, too, are a kind of 'no win, no fee' arrangement. In such cases, the lawyer usually receives a percentage of the damages awarded to their client.[16]

9-) What is the destination of civil appeals?

The Civil Division of the Court of Appeal is the body that deals with appeals from all Divisions of the High Court, certain appeals from the County Courts and those from some tribunals. The Master of the Rolls is the President of the Civil Division. Either the Court of Appeal or a lower court grants 'permission' for an appeal. While a single Lord Chief Justice usually grants permission to appeal, full appeals are heard before two or three judges. The Civil Division of the Court Appeal is also responsible for hearing family cases.[17]

---

[16] Thomas and McGourlay, pp. 235, 236.
[17] Courts & Tribunals Judiciary, https://www.judiciary.uk/about-the-judiciary/the-justice-system/jurisdictions/civil-jurisdiction/ (accessed 1 February 2021).

10-) What is 'Alternative Dispute Resolution' (ADR)?

ADR is an alternative way of resolving a dispute between parties (claimant and respondent). It avoids going to courts or tribunals. According to the glossary to the CPR 1998, ADR is "collective description of methods of resolving disputes otherwise than through the normal trial process."

11-) What are the forms of ADR? What are the advantages and disadvantages of each form of ADR?

The most common forms of ADR are adjudication, arbitration, conciliation, mediation and negotiation.[18]

Forms of ADR	Description	Pros	Cons
Adjudication	This type of ADR is usually only used for disputes arising from construction contracts.	It is a flexible process. Cost effective. Decision is final and legally binding.	If experts disagree, it might not be a cost-effective type of ADR. In the event that the adjudication agreement does not stipulate that the decision of the adjudicator will be final and binding on both parties, there may be a need for further litigation or arbitration, meaning increased costs.
Arbitration	Arbitrators are appointed by the parties concerned to resolve disputes over a contract.	The parties have the opportunity to select an arbitrator with the expertise and experience necessary.	It might not be a cost-effective option if a process resembling a trial is used. The parties have to accept the decision of an arbitrator, even if

---

[18] Thomas and McGourlay, pp. 204-205. See also Wilson, S., Rutherford, H. & Storey, T., *English Legal System*, 2. Edition, Oxford University Press, 2016; Porter Dodson Solicitors & Advisors, 'Alternative Dispute Resolution', https://www.porterdodson.co.uk/alternative-dispute-resolution-solicitors#:~:text = Negotiation,a%20meeting%20between%20all%20concerned (accessed 1 February 2021); Rocket Lawyer, 'Alternative Dispute Resolution', https://www.rocketlawyer.com/gb/en/quick-guides/alternative-dispute-resolution (accessed 1 February 2021).

Forms of ADR	Description	Pros	Cons
Arbitration (cont.)		This is a confidential process with no public access. When parties launch arbitration proceedings, the arbitrator is granted the power to resolve the dispute. In the event the parties are not happy with the decision of the arbitrator, there is no way they can challenge it, since it is binding (like a court judgment). In the absence of an arbitration clause, parties are still able to agree to resolve the dispute through arbitration. It is possible to design the process for a specific place. If resolution is based on written submissions it can be straightforward and low in cost.	they disagree with it. If a party is not happy with the process the arbitrator does not have broad powers, as possessed by a judge, to ensure co-operation.

Forms of ADR	Description	Pros	Cons
Conciliation	Conciliation is arranged by a 'conciliator', an unbiased, neutral person. They assist both parties to reach a solution that everyone is happy with. Conciliation is a process commonly used in employment situations, but not in commercial disputes. Conciliation is a process that an individual must engage in prior to taking a claim to the Employment Tribunal.	It is carried out confidentially and without bias. Cost-effective. Enables parties to see how the other party sees things. A good option when the parties are still on good terms.	In the event of the process failing, costs will mount due to an additional procedure.

Forms of ADR	Description	Pros	Cons
Mediation	Mediation is a form of process in which an impartial third party, the mediator, assists the parties to reach an agreement that is acceptable to both. Family disputes often use mediation as privacy is particularly important. This is also the case in commercial disputes. Companies may be reluctant to reveal sensitive information regarding their business operations or have concerns about their reputation. Even if a company wins a case, the media may twist things and expose errors the company has made.	It is private and confidential and not open to the public. Mediation is a more flexible way of, for instance, re-negotiating a clause in a contract. One party may apologise, or lower the price of a contract, or make an offer of free services. Cost effective. Speedier than a hearing in Court. There is flexibility in that mediation can be organised when and where is convenient for both parties. It is more informal than a court and less confrontational.	Legal aid is not available. Mediators and arbitrators may not comprehend complicated legislation that is in dispute if they are not lawyers. Imbalance of power: one of the parties may have more going for them, for instance, *an employer v an employee*, leading to an exploitative situation. There is no tenet of precedent: as decisions are not notified there is no source for future cases to refer to.

Forms of ADR	Description	Pros	Cons
Negotiation	Negotiation involves the parties and their lawyers looking to reach agreement either by an exchange of written correspondence or a meeting of all parties to resolve a dispute.	A flexible process utilised by the parties and/or their lawyers. Cost effective. Clients instruct their lawyers and keep absolute control of the conclusion by approving agreements.	A client may not achieve the result they are seeking if the best aspects of a case are not properly explained. The informal nature of the process may be confusing. It may not work if parties have impractical expectations.

A SAMPLE ESSAY TYPE QUESTION:

"Skilled mediators are now able to achieve results satisfactory to both parties in many cases which are quite beyond the power of lawyers and courts to achieve. This court has knowledge of cases where intense feelings have arisen, for instance in relation to clinical negligence claims. But when the parties are brought together on neutral soil with a skilled mediator to help them resolve their differences, it may very well be that the mediator is able to achieve a result by which the parties shake hands at the end and feel that they have gone away having settled the dispute on terms with which they are happy to live. A mediator may be able to provide solutions which are beyond the powers of the court to provide." *(Brooke LJ Dunnett v Railtrack plc (Practice Note) [2002] 1 WLR 2434)*

Discuss whether mediation should be a compulsory step before applying to court.

There are two ways of answering this question.

Yes, mediation should be obligatory:

- Mediation is more cost-effective than going to court and would therefore be less costly for both the parties and the tax payer;

- Mediation assists reconciliation between parties;
- Parties are able to select ways to settle their dispute with mediation;
- Mediation is compulsory in many disputes in the US, Australia and Canada;
- Mediation would help to reduce the backlog of claims that has built up in the court system;
- Dreadon notes: "Even where a party is initially unwilling to participate, surprising results can be achieved with the aid of skilful and experienced mediator. Further, mediations can be set up very quickly and parties are free to leave at any time, so concerns about the obstruction of a party's right of access to the court would appear to be misconceived";[19]
- Married couples who wish to divorce have to attend a mediation meeting prior to applying to court.

No, mediation should not be compulsory:

- Mediation is a voluntary process. Wilson, Rutherford & Storey give two reasons for this:
  o If mediation were compulsory, barriers would emerge between the parties and the mediator, which would hinder the negotiation process; and
  o Compromise is the usual outcome in a mediation process (a win/win). Compulsory mediation would probably hinder reaching an agreement and might drag out the dispute to the financial detriment of the parties.[20]

- In *Hasley v Milton Keynes General NHS Trust [2004] EWCA Civ 576*, the Court of Appeal remarked that forcing parties into mediation might involve preventing litigants having access to court, which could consequently contravene Art 6(1) of the ECHR (right to a fair trial).
- No precedent can be established, which could lead to uncertainty. Having a court hearing means there is some certainty as regards the result of the case.

---

[19] Dreadon, K., 'Mediation Order', (2005) 149 SJ 12. See also Wilson, Rutherford & Storey, p. 570.
[20] Wilson, Rutherford & Storey, p.568.

CHAPTER VI

THE CRIMINAL JUSTICE SYSTEM

Learning Outcomes:

In this chapter, you should be able to understand:

- ✓ the functions of the courts in the criminal justice system;
- ✓ the fundamental features of criminal litigation;
- ✓ the main tenets followed by the criminal courts;
- ✓ the different kinds of process in criminal litigation.

Questions and Answers:

1-) What does the criminal justice system involve?

The criminal law formalises criminal offences and the regulations and procedures that are followed when the police investigate an offence that they allege you have committed. It also lays down what happens when you are charged, and when you are to attend a criminal court. In the event of your admitting the offence or if you are found guilty, the court will sentence you, the penalties available being fines, community orders or imprisonment.[1]

2-) What regulates the criminal justice system?

Criminal Procedure Rules 2015 is a procedural code whose overriding aim is to provide criminal procedure as well as to enable the criminal courts (Court of Appeal -Criminal Division; Crown and Magistrates' Courts) to deal with cases justly.[2]

---

[1] The Law Society, 'Criminal law', https://www.lawsociety.org.uk/en/public/for-public-visitors/common-legal-issues/criminal-law (accessed 1 February 2021).
[2] The Criminal Procedure Rules 2015, https://www.legislation.gov.uk/uksi/2015/1490/contents/made (accessed 1 February 2021).

3-) What is the court hierarchy in the criminal justice system? What are their functions?

Criminal Courts

Supreme Court (formerly House of Lords)

Court of Appeal (Criminal Division)

Crown Courts/Magistrates' Courts

Supreme Court: The final court of appeal for all cases, including criminal cases, in the entire UK.[3]

Court of Appeal (Criminal Division): It is one of two divisions of the Court of Appeal of England and Wales. This court deals with appeals relating to cases heard in the Crown Court. For example,

- convictions in the Crown Court;
- sentences given by the Crown Court (even if the conviction was in a Magistrate's Court);
- confiscation orders imposed by the Crown Court

It also deals with applications for permission ('leave') to appeal judgments handed down in all these courts.

Moreover, it also deals with other kinds of appeal regarding Crown Court cases, including cases referred by the Attorney General when concern exists that an over-lenient sentence has been handed down by the Crown Court.

The court also deals with appeals against judgments handed down by 'service courts' (military courts) and is called the 'Court Martial Appeal Court' when this occurs.[4]

Crown Court: These courts hear serious criminal cases, for instance:

- murder;
- rape;
- robbery.

---

[3] See the Supreme Court website: www.supremecourt.uk.
[4] 'Court of Appeal Criminal Division', https://www.gov.uk/courts-tribunals/court-of-appeal-criminal-division (accessed 1 February 2021).

And also hear:

- appeals against a Magistrates' Court conviction or sentence;
- cases passed from a Magistrates' Court for trial or sentencing.

A Crown Court usually features a jury – responsible for deciding if you are guilty or not - and a judge who is responsible for passing sentence. The judge has a broad selection of sentences, including community sentences and prison sentences (with a maximum of life sentences).[5]

Magistrates' Court: All criminal cases commence in Magistrates' Courts. Cases in these courts are dealt with by 2 or 3 magistrates or a district judge. Magistrates' Courts do not have juries. A Magistrates' Court generally deals with cases called 'summary offences' such as:

- most motoring offences;
- minor criminal damage;
- common assault (not causing significant injury).

It can also hear more serious offences such as:

- burglary;
- drugs offences.

Such offences are referred to as 'either way' offences, which can be dealt with either in a Magistrates' Court or a Crown Court. The defendant is given the choice of either a summary trial in the Magistrates' Court or a trial in the Crown Court involving an indictment.

Magistrates' Courts have to refer 'indictable offences' (the most grave offences) to the Crown Court, for instance:

- murder;
- rape;
- robbery.

A Magistrates' Court is able to hand down penalties such as:

- up to 6 months in prison (or up to 12 months in total for more than one offence);
- a fine of up to £5,000;
- a community sentence, like doing unpaid work in the community;
- a ban, for example, from driving or keeping an animal.

---

[5] Ibid.

A combination of penalties may also be given - for instance, a fine and unpaid work in the community.[6]

Youth Court: A Youth Court is a specific form of Magistrates' Court for minors aged between 10 and 17. A Youth Court consists of either: 3 magistrates or a district judge. Youth Courts do not have juries. A Youth Court handles cases such as:

- theft and burglary;
- anti-social behaviour;
- drugs offences.

Cases involving serious offences, such as murder or rape, begin in the Youth Court but are referred to a Crown Court. The Youth Court has a variety of options, including a range of penalties such as:

- Community sentences;
- Detention and Training Orders carried out in secure centres for young people.[7]

4-) Who are the parties in the criminal justice system?

The Prosecutor: The party that brings criminal proceedings against a person.

The Defendant: The party defending the case.

5-) What is the process in the criminal justice system?

Criminal cases are usually heard in court after the Crown Prosecution Service has decided to prosecute an individual for committing an alleged offence. Over 95 per cent of cases are heard in Magistrates' Courts, where magistrates listen to the evidence and decide whether a person is guilty or innocent. In cases of a more serious nature the evidence will be heard by a district judge (Magistrates' Court) or a circuit judge in the Crown Court, where a jury trial will take place. Particularly grave criminal cases, like murder and rape, may go before a High Court judge.

Both magistrates and judges have the authority to impose prison sentences, if the gravity of the offence warrants it. However, there are other options. A judge or magistrate may hand down a community punishment, or a control order that limits a person's movements or activities. When deciding

---

[6] Ibid.
[7] Ibid.

on a sentence, a judge will take into consideration the effect a particular sentence might have on an individual re-offending.[8]

6-) What is the trial process in the criminal justice system?

Prior to the commencement of a criminal trial a judge will go through the case papers in order to get a good understanding of the case. Amongst these papers are the indictment setting out the charges which the defendant is facing, witness statements and documentation of applications that parties to the trial might make regarding the admissibility of evidence.

In jury trials at the Crown Court, the judge supervises the process of selecting and swearing in the jury, directing jurors about their role as to weighing the facts and reaching a decision. The judge also warns jurors not to discuss the trial with anyone apart from the other jurors while in court.

During the trial

After the trial has started the judge is careful to give all parties involved the opportunity to set out their case and for it to be considered in the best possible way. The judge supervises the way the trial proceeds to ensure it accords with relevant law and practice. The judge takes notes as evidence is presented and decides on legal questions, for instance, the admissibility of evidence.

When all evidence has been presented the judge sums up, making plain for the jury what the law is for each of the charges and what the prosecution has to prove in order for the jury to be certain. The judge uses the notes made during the trial to remind the jury of key points, emphasising the strengths and weaknesses of the argument made by each party. Finally, the judge directs the jury as to their duties and the jurors go to the jury deliberation room to make their decision.

Sentencing

If the jury reaches a guilty verdict, the judge will decide on a sentence that is appropriate. There are various factors that come into play: mainly the circumstances of the case, the effect the crime has had on the victim, and relevant law, in particular, Court of Appeal judgments. The judge will also take into account any reports and references on the defendant as mitigation. After the judge has weighed up all these factors the sentence or penalty will be declared.[9]

---

[8] Courts and Tribunals Judiciary, 'Criminal Justice', https://www.judiciary.uk/about-the-judiciary/the-justice-system/jurisdictions/criminal-jurisdiction/ (accessed 1 February 2021).
[9] Ibid.

7-) What is the destination of criminal appeals?

The Criminal Division of the Court of Appeal. Criminal Division judges deal with appeals in criminal cases from the Crown Court. The Lord Chief Justice is President of the Court of Appeal Criminal Division. There is also a Vice President who lends support. The bench in the Criminal Division usually has a Lord or Lady Justice and two High Court judges.[10]

8-) Who are the main stakeholders in the criminal justice system?

Court of Appeal (Criminal Division): One of the two divisions of the Court of Appeal of England and Wales.

HM Courts & Tribunals Service: This body is responsible for the administration of all criminal, civil and Family Courts and Tribunals in England and Wales.

Her Majesty's Crown Prosecution Service Inspectorate: It examines the CPS and other prosecuting agencies. Its objective is to improve the quality of justice and help prosecution services to become more efficient, effective and fair.

Her Majesty's Prison & Probation Service: Responsible for seeing that sentences handed down by the courts are carried out, both in custody and the community, and for the rehabilitation of offenders through education and employment.

Magistrates' Courts hear less serious criminal offences. **Youth courts** are a special type of Magistrates' Courts.

Supreme Court: The ultimate court of appeal for the whole of the UK.

The Crown Court hears the most serious offences.

The Crown Prosecution Service (CPS): This institution is responsible for initiating prosecutions into criminal cases investigated by the police and other investigative bodies in England and Wales.

The Home Office: The main government department, with a wide range of responsibilities, including immigration, passports, policy on drugs, crime, fire services, counter-terrorism and the police.

The Law Officers: The Attorney General acts as chief legal adviser to the government and oversees the Crown Prosecution Service and the Serious Fraud Office. The Attorney General is also responsible for the Government Legal Department and Her Majesty's Crown Prosecution Service

---

[10] Ibid.

Inspectorate, and carries out several independent functions of public interest. The Solicitor General supports the Attorney in all these duties.

The Ministry of Justice: It oversees the various elements of the justice system – the courts, prisons, probation services and attendance centres. Its functions cover criminal, civil and family justice, democracy, rights and the constitution. The Ministry of Justice is a ministerial department, backed by 32 agencies and public bodies.

The Police: In England and Wales there are 43 police forces that undertake the investigation of crime, collect evidence and arrest or detain suspects. When a suspect is apprehended, in less serious cases the police either issue a caution, take no further action, issue a fixed penalty notice or refer the matter to the CPS. When the case is serious, the police send the files to the CPS for them to make a decision as to whether to prosecute. [11]

9-) What do costs in the civil justice system involve?

The planned budget for the UK's Ministry of Justice in 2020/21 is £8.3 billion.[12] Individuals who are charged with a criminal offence may be eligible for legal aid. If this is the case, a government agency - the Legal Aid Agency - will pay all, or some, of the person's legal fees to their solicitor. Legal aid is means-tested, that is, the amount a person receives is dependent on their income and assets, if any. Legal aid is also dependant on the offence in question and the court that will hear the case. People who have been charged may have to make a contribution towards their legal expenses. If they do not qualify for legal aid, they can instruct a solicitor, but will have to meet the cost themselves.[13]

10-) Is there any legal aid in the criminal justice system? Is there any alternative way to access criminal justice?

According to Article 6(3)(c) of the HRA 1998 (Article 6(3)(c) of the ECHR), "everyone charged with a criminal offence has the following minimum rights: …to defend himself in person or through legal assistance of his own choosing or, if he has not sufficient means to pay for legal assistance, to be given it free when the interests of justice so require…"

Legal aid is an important source to access criminal justice (See Legal Aid, Sentencing and Punishment of Offenders Act -LASPO- 2012). Any person

---

[11] CPS, 'The Criminal Justice System', https://www.cps.gov.uk/about-cps/criminal-justice-system (accessed 1 February 2021).
[12] HM Treasury, 'Policy Paper Budget 2020', 12 March 2020, https://www.gov.uk/government/publications/budget-2020-documents/budget-2020 (accessed 1 February 2021).
[13] The Law Society, https://www.lawsociety.org.uk/en/public/for-public-visitors/common-legal-issues/criminal-law (accessed 1 February 2021).

aged under 16 (or under 18 if in full-time education) involved in any criminal activity is automatically entitled to legal aid for representation in court. The same is true for those on certain benefits.[14] The Legal Aid Agency is an executive agency of the Ministry of Justice dealing with criminal aid in England and Wales *(See Chapter V for the Agency's objectives)*.[15]

Legal aid is available for criminal proceedings (Section 14 LASPO 2012) including criminal trials, sentencing hearings, appeals, and advice and assistance pre-trial (Section 15 LASPO 2012). According to Section 17 LASPO 2012, the following factors must be taken into account in deciding what the interests of justice consist of for the purposes of such a determination:

a) whether, if any matter arising in the proceedings is decided against the individual, the individual would be likely to lose his or her liberty or livelihood or to suffer serious damage to his or her reputation,

b) whether the determination of any matter arising in the proceedings may involve consideration of a substantial question of law,

c) whether the individual may be unable to understand the proceedings or to state his or her own case,

d) whether the proceedings may involve the tracing, interviewing or expert cross-examination of witnesses on behalf of the individual, and

e) whether it is in the interests of another person that the individual be represented.

In addition, there are other alternative sources such as the Citizen Advice Bureau, law centres and pro bono which can be used to access criminal justice. Or, alternatively, you can use your own resources, such as a traditional retainer, to access justice.

Please note that the term 'traditional retainer' denotes a client paying for his/her own case without support from the public authorities or other benefactors.[16]

11-) How does the jury system function in the criminal justice system?

Juries hear criminal cases in the Crown Court, and are also present at Coroner Inquests and Defamation trials. They consist of twelve jurors who

---

[14] Legal aid, https://www.gov.uk/legal-aid/eligibility (accessed 1 February 2021).
[15] Legal Aid Agency, https://assets.publishing.service.gov.uk/government/uploads/system/uploads/attachment_data/file/902746/Legal_Aid_Agency_annual_report_and_accounts_2019_to_2020.pdf (accessed 1 February 2021).
[16] Thomas and McGourlay, p. 235.

are selected at random from the electoral register *(For further information see Chapter VII)*.

A SAMPLE CASE ANALYSIS TYPE QUESTION:

Part One – Section 8 Theft Act 1968 – Robbery

(1) A person is guilty of robbery if he steals, and immediately before or at the time of doing so, and in order to do so, he uses force on any person or puts or seeks to put any person in fear of being then and there subjected to force.

(2) A person guilty of robbery, or of an assault with intent to rob, shall on conviction on indictment be liable to imprisonment for life.

Please read Section 8 and consider whether robbery has been committed in the following scenarios.

Firstly, you should analyse the key element of Section 8:

1. Steals

2. Uses force on any person

    or

    puts any person in fear of being then and there subjected to force

    or

    seeks to put any person in fear of being then and there subjected to force

3. In order to steal

4. Immediately before or at the time of stealing.

Secondly, you should apply the law to the following cases:

1. **There are three people waiting at a bus stop. Anna, Leyanda and James. Anna is having a conversation on her mobile phone. James suddenly takes hold of Leyanda's arm, bends it behind her back and says to Anna 'Give me that mobile or I'll break her arm.' Anna, who does not know Leyanda, hands James the phone and James dashes away.**

A robbery has taken place. James has stolen a mobile phone. He has used force on Leyanda, who is defined as any person. The words 'any person'

69

make absolutely clear that the force in question does not need to be inflicted on the person whose property is being stolen, or that the person who is the victim of force does not need to be a friend or acquaintance of the person whose property is being stolen.

James exercised this force just before stealing and did it so that he could steal.

Anna in all probability gave James the mobile in order to protect Leyanda, but there is no need for this causal link in Section 8.

Ensure all four elements needed to prove robbery have been thoroughly examined and that the importance of this has been understood.

2. **Alex is on a train. Sitting opposite him is Helen. Her handbag is on the table between them. There is only one other person in the whole carriage. As the train pulls into a station, Alex leans over and whispers to Helen 'Give me your bag, if you make a fuss, I'll hit you in the face'. Helen is deaf and cannot hear what Alex says. She smiles at Alex, who stands up, snatches her handbag and gets off the train.**

A robbery has taken place. Alex has taken the bag and before doing so he tried to put Helen in fear of being then and there subjected to force. It is irrelevant that he did not actually use any force or that Helen was not frightened that he would.

3. **Max steals Leyanda's wallet when she is purchasing a train ticket. On the same day Leyanda sees Max queuing in a supermarket and attempts to grab his arm. Max kicks out at Leyanda, catching her in the leg, and flees.**

No robbery has taken place, although Max has stolen Leyanda's wallet. He has used force on Leyanda, but the force was not used before or at the time of stealing. Moreover, he did not use the force to carry out the theft.

4. Abi encounters Danial, who is with his dog, Poppy, in the park. Helen takes Poppy into her arms and places a knife to the dog's throat, saying threateningly 'Either you give me your wallet or the dog's had it.' Danial complies and hands Helen his wallet.

What has taken place here is not robbery. Despite the fact Helen has stolen Danial's wallet and threatened to use force immediately before stealing and to be able to steal, she has not used force, or made any person fear that force might be used, nor has she tried to make any person fear the use of force. Causing a person (Danial) to fear that a dog, or even another person, would be subjected to force is not part of Section 8.

5. Alex utters insults to Matthew. He reacts, punching Alex in the face. Consequently, Alex's wallet falls from his pocket. Matthew picks it up and dashes away with it.

Matthew has stolen Alex's wallet. He has also used force on Alex immediately before stealing the wallet. However, this does not qualify as a robbery since the intention of the force had nothing to do with the taking of the wallet.

CHAPTER VII

LEGAL PROFESSIONALS IN THE ENGLISH LEGAL SYSTEM

Learning Outcomes:

In this chapter, you should be able to understand:

- ✓ the legal professionals;
- ✓ the difference between solicitors and barristers;
- ✓ the functions of juries;
- ✓ the appointment of judges.

Questions and Answers:

1-) Who are the key personnel in the English Legal System?

Attorney General; Barristers; Court Clerks; Court Ushers; Judges; Jury; Justice Secretary/Lord Chancellor; Magistrates; Legal Advisor; Legal Executives; Lord Chief Justice; Paralegals; Prosecutors; Solicitors and Solicitor General.

2-) What are their functions?

Attorney General: The Attorney General is the main legal adviser to the Crown and the Government and has several other independent public interest functions, in addition to supervising the Law Officers' departments.[1]

Barristers: Members of the Bar. A barrister usually offers specialist legal advice and represents both individuals and organisations in courts and tribunals, in addition to providing written legal advice. A barrister's role is to undertake advocacy in court; instruct regarding the merits of a case; offer guidance on points of law; give advice on offers to settle; draft proceedings and carry out research. Their regulatory body is the Bar Standards Board, which is a part of the Legal Services Board. Barristers with at least ten years' experience may apply to become Queen's Counsel. QCs take on particularly

---

[1] 'Ministerial role: Attorney General', https://www.gov.uk/government/ministers/attorney-general (accessed 1 February 2021).

important work and are called 'silks' on account of the Courts' gown that they wear. When there is a king on the throne they are known as King's Counsel.[2]

Court Clerks: They are responsible for administrative duties in the criminal and civil justice systems, like maintaining court records, overseeing witnesses and jurors swearing oaths, and certifying copies of court orders and judgments using the court's seal.[3]

Court Ushers: Their responsibility is to ensure that all those involved with a court case are present and familiar with the proceedings and their part in it.[4]

Judges: An official whose task is to oversee court proceedings.

> **Circuit judge:** A judge who sits in the County Court and/or the Crown Court.

> **District judge:** A judicial officer of the Magistrates' Court whose duties involve hearing applications made within proceedings and final hearings subject to any limit of jurisdiction.

> **Justices:** Judges who sit in the High Court of Justice.

> **Law Lords:** The judges who sit in the Supreme Court.

> **Lord Justice of Appeal:** Title given to certain judges who sit in the Court of Appeal.

> **Master:** Judicial officer of the High Court in the Royal Courts of Justice who normally deals with preliminary matters before trial.

> **Master of the Rolls:** Senior civil judge in the Court of Appeal.

Jury: A panel of ordinary citizens that hears a criminal (or sometimes a civil) trial. A jury is made up of 12 jurors.[5]

Justice Secretary/Lord Chancellor: The cabinet minister responsible for the Ministry of Justice.[6]

---

[2] Slater Gordon Lawyers, 'Difference between a lawyer, a solicitor & a barrister', https://www.slatergordon.co.uk/newsroom/difference-between-a-lawyer-a-solicitor-and-a-barrister-explained/ (accessed 1 February 2021).
[3] Alla about careers, 'Court Clerk', https://www.allaboutcareers.com/careers/job-profile/court-clerk (accessed 1 February 2021).
[4] National Careers Service, 'Court usher', https://nationalcareers.service.gov.uk/job-profiles/court-usher (accessed 1 February 2021).
[5] 'Jury service', https://www.gov.uk/jury-service (accessed 1 February 2021).
[6] 'Ministerial role: Lord Chancellor and Secretary of State for Justice', https://www.gov.uk/government/ministers/secretary-of-state-for-justice (accessed 1 February 2021).

Magistrates: Magistrates deal with cases in courts in the area where they reside. They work on a voluntary basis. They hear cases in both the criminal court and the family court.[7]

Legal Adviser: Court legal advisers are qualified lawyers who issue advice to magistrates and district judges regarding the law.[8]

Legal Executives: Legal executives are specialists in one field of law and function in a similar way to solicitors. Their regulatory body is the ILEX Professional Standards Board which is a part of the Legal Services Board.[9]

Lord Chief Justice: The head of the Judiciary in England and Wales. Also serves as the President of the Courts of England and Wales and informs Parliament and the Government of the opinions of the judiciary.[10]

Paralegals: Paralegals conduct research, draw up legal documents and advise clients.[11]

Prosecutors: The prosecutor co-operates with the police in order to construct a case supporting a charge that reflects the gravity of the crime perpetrated by the accused.[12]

Solicitors: Qualified lawyers who mainly advise clients and prepare their cases. Their duties involve informing individuals and organisations about the law, and they also carry out work such as representing and/or defending the legal rights of a client. Their regulatory body is the Solicitors Regulation Authority, which is a part of the Legal Services Board. [13]

Solicitor General: The Solicitor General's role is to support the Attorney General in all his responsibilities.[14]

---

[7] 'Become a magistrate', https://www.gov.uk/become-magistrate (accessed 1 February 2021).
[8] National Careers Service, 'Court Legal Adviser', https://nationalcareers.service.gov.uk/job-profiles/court-legal-adviser (accessed 1 February 2021).
[9] National Careers Service, 'Legal Executive', https://nationalcareers.service.gov.uk/job-profiles/legal-executive (accessed 1 February 2021).
[10] UK Parliament, 'Lord Chief Justice', https://www.parliament.uk/site-information/glossary/lord-chief-justice/ (accessed 1 February 2021).
[11] National Careers Service, 'Paralegal', https://nationalcareers.service.gov.uk/job-profiles/paralegal (accessed 1 February 2021).
[12] CPS, 'The Prosecutors' Pledge', https://www.cps.gov.uk/prosecutors-pledge (accessed 1 February 2021).
[13] Slater Gordon Lawyers, https://www.slatergordon.co.uk/newsroom/difference-between-a-lawyer-a-solicitor-and-a-barrister-explained/ (accessed 1 February 2021).
[14] 'Ministerial role: Solicitor General', https://www.gov.uk/government/ministers/solicitor-general (accessed 1 February 2021).

3-) What is the difference between solicitors and barristers?

SOLICITORS	BARRISTERS
Qualifying as a Solicitor: • Complete law degree- LLB or GDL; • Legal Practice Course; • 2 years training contract as a 'trainee solicitor'. **Progression:** • Partner; • Judiciary. **Regulator:** • Solicitors Regulation Authority; • The Law Society represents solicitors' interests. **Roles:** • To advise individuals and organisations on the law; • Most solicitors specialise in one area of law e.g. family law, commercial law, litigation etc; • Solicitors can gain higher rights of audience to appear in the higher courts; • And will be involved in contentious or non-contentious work: Contentious matters refer to issues that might entail a legal dispute, for instance, an employee wishing to sue their employer for unfair dismissal, a company wishing to claim compensation from another company for late provision of goods, personal injury claims, criminal proceedings. Non-contentious work is everything else such as advising a company on a merger with another company, purchasing commercial property, listing on the stock exchange, drawing up a will.	**Qualifying as a Barrister:** • Qualifying law degree- LLB or GDL; • BPTC (Before starting this course, a person must join one of the four Inns of Court: Middle Temple; Inner Temple; Lincoln's Inn and Gray's Inn); • Pupillage. **Progression:** • Queen's Counsel (QCs) – the elite advocates; • Judiciary. **Regulator:** • The Bar Standards Board regulates barristers; • The Bar Council represents the interests of barristers. **Roles:** • Primarily to undertake advocacy at court; • Barristers may work in all areas of law e.g. commercial, criminal, intellectual property, employment law; • Advise on merits of the case; • Advising on points of law; • Advising on offers to settle; • Drafting proceedings; • Research. **Place of work:** Barristers are usually self-employed and operate in chambers where they share branding, administrative facilities and staff (clerks). Barristers sometimes work for local government or the Crown Prosecution Service or are directly employed by a company.

Place of work:	
In general, solicitors work for law firms that are owned and run by partners. Solicitors work in all kinds of law firms: high-street, regional, national and international firms. Some solicitors work in-house or as sole practitioners.	

4-) Do you think solicitors and barristers should be merged together?

There are two different ways of engaging with this question:

Yes, it would be advantageous for them to be merged:

- In lots of countries there is no such split in the profession;
- The differences between the roles of solicitors and barristers have become obscured. There is a certain overlap in the work of solicitors and barristers. All solicitors are able to act on behalf of clients in County Courts, Magistrates' Courts and Employment Tribunals. Employment law solicitors also routinely take on advocacy at tribunals. Some solicitors apply for higher rights of audience (the right of a solicitor to conduct proceedings in a court), allowing them to represent clients in the senior courts.

No, it would not be beneficial for them to be merged:

- Barristers are trained in advocacy and are skilled in this role. They are not authorised to issue proceedings (that is the role of the solicitor) emphasising that their role is to focus on advocacy;
- Since barristers are more detached from clients, they are able to be more objective;
- Barristers' fees are usually lower because they have fewer expenses. This leads to more efficient and economic representation in court;
- The public need the services of a solicitor to instruct a barrister, as the public has little knowledge of law and types of barrister. Solicitors have the expertise to select an appropriate barrister to represent the client in court;
- It makes for a more competitive arena;
- It provides better access to justice through barristers who specialise in advocacy at court.[15]

---

[15] Wilson, Rutherford & Storey, p. 302.

5-) Who appoints the judges? What is the application process?

Since April 2006, an independent Judicial Appointments Commission consisting of 15 members has supervised judicial appointments (CRA 2005, Schedule 12).

All appointments are made through open competition, a fair, transparent procedure. The Commission makes recommendations regarding candidates to the Lord Chancellor, who has three options (CRA 2005, Section 94C):

- ✓ Accept the recommendation;
- ✓ Reject the recommendation;
- ✓ Ask the Panel to reconsider the selection.

The Commission also has a duty to "encourage diversity in the range of persons available for selection for appointments". The objective of this is to broaden the pool of candidates and then make appointments on merit. The Commission includes judges, but they do not constitute a majority or act as representatives, and the Commission has a chair who is a layperson.[16]

The Application Processes:[17]

6-) What is the eligibility criteria? How are members of the judiciary removed?

Eligibility:

Only citizens (including people with dual nationality) of the UK, the Republic of Ireland or a Commonwealth country may apply to be a judge. There is no age restriction for candidates, except the statutory retirement

---

[16] Courts and Tribunals Judiciary, 'Judicial appointments', https://www.judiciary.uk/about-the-judiciary/the-judiciary-the-government-and-the-constitution/jud-acc-ind/jud-appts/ (accessed 1 February 2021).
[17] The Judicial Appointments Commission, 'Guidance on the application process', https://judicial appointments.gov.uk/guidance-on-the-application-process-2/ (accessed 1 February 2021).

age of 70 for all judges. The majority of judicial posts ask for a legal qualification possessed for at least five or seven years.[18]

Removal:

Both Houses of Parliament may petition the Crown to request the removal of a judge of the High Court or the Court of Appeal. However, this power has never needed to be exercised in England and Wales.

The Lord Chancellor may remove Circuit and District Judges on the grounds of 'misbehaviour' or 'incapacity'. However, he needs the agreement of the Lord Chief Justice to do so (See section 11(3) of the Supreme Court Act 1981).[19]

7-) How does the jury system work in the criminal justice system?

Juries are a feature, both of criminal cases in the Crown Court, and also of Coroner Inquests and Defamation trials. A jury consists of twelve jurors who are selected randomly from the electoral register. Jurors are independent of parliament, government and the judiciary. It is their responsibility to establish the facts of a case (following directions from the judge on the law) before reaching a verdict. The judge asks the jury to reach a guilty (convicted) or not guilty (acquitted) verdict. While a verdict ideally should be unanimous, the judge will accept a majority verdict of 10-2 (Section 17 Juries Act 1974).

Section 17 states that

> (1) Subject to subsections (3) and (4) below, the verdict of a jury in proceedings in the Crown Court or the High Court need not be unanimous if - (a)in a case where there are not less than eleven jurors, ten of them agree on the verdict; and (b)in a case where there are ten jurors, nine of them agree on the verdict...

It is an unpaid service, but jurors may receive payments for travelling and subsistence; and for financial loss (Section 19). Eligibility rules are contained in Section 1 of the Juries Act 1974:

- Registered as an elector;
- Aged between 18-76; and

---

[18] Courts and Tribunals Judiciary, 'Becoming a judge', https://www.judiciary.uk/about-the-judiciary/judges-career-paths/becoming-a-judge/ (accessed 1 February 2021).
[19] Courts and Tribunals Judiciary, 'Judges and Parliament', https://www.judiciary.uk/about-the-judiciary/the-judiciary-the-government-and-the-constitution/jud-acc-ind/judges-and-parliament/#:~:text=Both%20Houses%20of%20Parliament%20have,or%20the%20Court%20of%20Appeal.&text=Circuit%20and%20District%20Judges%20can,the%20Lord%20Chief%20Justice%20agrees (accessed 1 February 2021).

- Ordinarily resident in the UK, Channel Islands or Isle of Man for 5 years from the age of 13. There is no requirement to be a British citizen;
- Not a mentally disordered as well as not a disqualified person;
- Certain groups were excluded from jury service such as doctors, judges, police, barristers, solicitors and mentally disordered persons (under the Mental Health Act 2013);
- Disqualification from jury service for:
  - Persons on bail; and
  - Persons sentenced to imprisonment:
  - More than 5 years imprisonment = life disqualification;
  - Up to 5 years = 10 years disqualification;
- Excusal from jury service under the Criminal Justice Act 2003:
  - Those who have already served on a jury in the last two years;
  - Members of the Armed Forces;
  - If you can show a 'good reason' (medical reasons, work, study etc.).[20]

8-) What are the advantages and disadvantages of having a jury system?

Advantages	Disadvantages
• It is important for ordinary people to be involved in the administration of justice by playing a role in determining a person's guilt, rather than the state doing this; • It is important for ordinary people to be involved in the administration of justice by playing a role in determining a person's guilt, rather than the state doing this; • Jurors are the best people to consider facts and what kind of behaviour should be considered	• It is costly and time-consuming; • There is a risk of jurors identifying with and feeling sympathy for the accused; • Prejudicial jurors – for example, there might be a risk of discrimination on the basis of race; • It is costly and time-consuming; • There is a risk of jurors identifying with and feeling sympathy for the accused; • Prejudicial jurors – for example, there might be a risk of discrimination on the basis of race;

---

[20] Juries Act 1974, Section 1, https://www.legislation.gov.uk/ukpga/1974/23/section/1 (accessed 1 February 2021); See also 'Jury Service', https://www.gov.uk/jury-service (accessed 1 February 2021); Gillespie and Weare, pp. 450-458, 477-485; Thomas and McGourlay, pp. 141-152.

Advantages	Disadvantages
correct, for instance, dishonest, rational etc.; • Having a clear separation of responsibility between adjudicators of the law and those who establish facts; • Enhances transparency and comprehension of the legal system for the public, the accused and the victim.	• Not addressing the task in a serious way *(See R v Qureshi [2001] EWCA Crim 1807, [2002] 1 WLR 518; R v Mirza [2004] UKHL 2, [2004] 1 AC 1118 cases)*; • Jurors not being able to fulfil the role, due to lack of legal skills or lack of legal knowledge hindering understanding of the evidence.

PRACTICE:

A-) Legal Professions of Solicitors, Barristers and Paralegals:

Alex is the owner of a building company that was engaged to construct exclusive apartments on land that had been purchased by Andrew's Estates. Andrew, who owns the property company, is a friend of Alex's. The two of them reached agreement on the project while on a night out. Andrew told Alex he would have a contract drafted, but he did not have it done.

After completing the first phase of construction, Alex has sent an invoice for £200K, as is the usual procedure. Andrew Estates claim that the work is poor, and, in the absence of a contract, that they have no liability to pay.

Alex intends to sue Andrew's estates and engages your firm. Your client wants to know what will be needed for this case. Examine the tasks listed below that are necessary. Determine who should carry out each task and explain what their role will be.

1. **Interviewing the client, receiving instructions and considering the legal questions in the case.**

   A solicitor who is a specialist in contract law will probably carry out the interview. Since legislation is constantly evolving and being updated, only a specialist solicitor would be able to deal with the case properly.

2. **Drafting preliminary witness statements, carrying out research as to whether a contract exists.**

   A paralegal would be capable of taking on this task, interviewing witnesses and doing research.

3. **Conducting negotiations for the client (negotiations fail – decision taken to launch proceedings in the High Court).**

Once more the solicitor will probably be tasked with handling this case.

4. **Drawing up court documents.**

Either the solicitor or paralegal could do this.

5. **Preparing a brief for counsel.**

The solicitor will summarise the case and pinpoint relevant issues relevant of the litigation.

6. **Evaluating the strength/weakness of the case and preparing the proposed Q&As for examining witnesses during the trial.**

Barristers represent clients in court and undertake the advocacy. They are tasked with presenting the legal case to the judge (and jury if present). The barrister must be knowledgeable on the points of law and be persuasive. Barristers are generally instructed by solicitors, but it is now possible for barristers to be instructed directly by clients. Barristers usually have a specialisation in certain areas of law when they begin to practice (indicated by the chambers that they join). As they gain experience, barristers will then specialise further and earn a reputation in that field.

7. **After hearing the trial, hands down judgment favouring the defendant.**

Since the amount at issue is high in this claim, a High Court Judge (Mr or Mrs Justice) will hear the case, addressed in court as 'my lord or my lady.'

B-) Jury system:

Can a conviction (guilty verdict) be overturned if the following circumstances apply:

(i) A juror makes a complaint that some other jurors did not listen to submissions during the trial?

No. In *R v Qureshi* the Court of Appeal ruled that these matters were safeguarded by Section 8 of the Contempt of Court Act 1981 which states "it is a contempt of court to obtain, disclose or solicit any particulars of statements made, opinions expressed, arguments advanced or votes cast by members of a jury in the course of their deliberations" *(R v Qureshi [2001] EWCA Crim 1807, [2002] 1 WLR 518).*

(ii) One of the jurors complains that other jurors showed bias towards the defendant because of his racial background?

No. This issue was considered by the House of Lords in *R v Mirza*. They disagreed with the Court of Appeal decision in *R v Qureshi*, declaring that Section 8 of the Contempt of Court Act 1981 is not relevant to the appeal courts. However, they stated that common law protected the confidentiality of discussions by the jury and that it was thus not possible to lodge an appeal against conviction based on allegations of inappropriate behaviour during deliberations.

If the juror had made the complaint before the jury had reached its verdict, then things might have been different (as in *Sander v UK* where the ECHR ruled that the judge should have dismissed the jury after a juror confessed to having made a comment of a racist nature) *(R v Mirza [2004] UKHL 2, [2004] 1 AC 1118; Sander v UK (2001) 31 EHRR 44).*

(iii) It comes to light that the jury had examined documents they had obtained themselves, in addition to the trial evidence?

Yes. It is apparent that the verdicts were not based solely on the evidence presented at trial. *R v Karayaka* involved a rape conviction. Academic documents on the subject of rape were found in the jury room. Hence, the conviction was quashed and an order issued for a retrial.

In the case of *R v Marshall & Crump,* unrelated material discovered in jury room after the trial had ended (printouts from the CPS, Home Office, and a criminal solicitors' firm website). The conviction was upheld after Hughes LJ stated that the documents in question were in the public domain, therefore members of the jury had legitimate access *(R v Karakaya [2005] EWCA Crim 346, [2005] 2 Cr App R 5.; R v Marshall & Crump [2007] EWCA Crim 35, [2007] Crim LR 562).*

(iv) It emerges that one of the jurors was a police officer who worked at the same police station as a prosecution witness?

In *R v Abdroikov, Green & Williamson*, Green's conviction was quashed on account of a juror being a police officer who had in the past worked at the same police station as the police officer who was a victim in the case. Since the case rested on a dispute over evidence between the defendant and the victim the majority found that it was likely the police officer juror would have believed a fellow officer. Abdroikov's conviction, however, was not overturned, as there was no link between the police officer on the jury and people involved in the case *(R v Abdroikov & Others [2007] UKHL 37, [2007] 1 WLR 2679).*

SUMMARY: SAMPLE TEST QUESTIONS

Source of Law (Domestic Legislation, Case Law and International Law)

1) Of the following definitions, which best describes common law?

   a. A body of law enshrined in Acts of Parliament.
   b. Particular rights, authority and immunities belonging to the Crown.
   c. Rules developed by judges in courts of law, not enacted by Parliament. ✓
   d. Decisions where courts use the authority of natural justice.

2) Of the following statements, which best describes delegated legislation?

   a. A law that a person or institution apart than Parliament creates, albeit with Parliamentary authority.
   b. A law that an individual or institution other than Parliament creates due to powers provided by the Privy Council.
   c. A law that an individual or institution other than Parliament makes by passing a specific kind of constitutional Act during a national crisis.
   d. A law made by an individual or organisation other than Parliament that is applicable solely in matters of environmental protection.

3) Which of the following would be considered secondary sources of European legislation?

   i.   Treaties
   ii. Regulations
   iii. Directives

   a. i. and ii. Only
   b. ii. and iii. Only
   c. i. and iii. Only
   d. All three

4) Which of the following most accurately describes the rule of language *expressio unius est exclusio alterius* used in statutory interpretation?

   a. When particular words come after general words, the general words are limited to the same types of objects.
   b. When one or more things of a class are expressly mentioned, others of the same class are excluded.
   c. When general words come after particular words, the general words are limited to the same kinds of objects.

d. If a list of items has no general words following it, the list will be considered to be incomplete.

5) Lord Justice Falcrone is sitting in the Court of Appeal. The case of *Wilson v Wilson* (decided in the House of Lords) has been handed to him as a binding precedent. However, Falcrone LJ has established that *Wilson v Wilson* is not binding for the Court of Appeal as regards the case he is now hearing. Consequently, it can be stated that Falcrone LJ has...

    a. reversed the decision in *Wilson v Wilson*.
    b. distinguished the decision in *Wilson v Wilson*.
    c. overruled the decision in *Wilson v Wilson*.
    d. affirmed the decision in *Wilson v Wilson*.

6) The European Convention on Human Rights was drawn up by the ...

    a. Council of Europe.
    b. European Council.
    c. European Commission.
    d. Council of Members.

7) Read the following sentence and select the correct answers from those listed in A – D.

Prior to the ____[1]_____ of the Human Rights Act 1998, individuals in England and Wales wanting to enforce their Convention rights had to travel to the _____[2]_____ located in ____[3]_____ to have their case heard.

    a. [1] enactment [2] European Court of Human Rights [3] Strasbourg
    b. [1] enactment [2] European Court of Justice [3] Strasbourg
    c. [1] coming into force [2] European Court of Human Rights [3] Strasbourg
    d. [1] coming into force [2] European Court of Justice [3] Brussels

8) Which of the following is NOT a rule of statutory construction?

    a. Ejusdem generis
    b. Res ipsa loquitur
    c. Noscitur a sociis
    d. Expressio unius exclusio alterius

9) Which one of the following best defines the legal term *ratio decidendi*?

    a. A judge's view of what the law should be.
    b. An incidental part of the judgment.

c. The legal basis of the decision.
d. The material facts leading to the decision.

10) Which of these is NOT technically an intrinsic aid to the interpretation of a statute?

a. Long title
b. Hansard
c. Short Title
d. Interpretation clause

11) Which of the following most accurately describes the effect of the legal maxim *stare decisis*?

a. When a court gives a decision in a case, any courts of a lower status to that court have to follow that verdict if the case they are hearing is similar, but courts of an equal standing do not necessarily have to follow it.

B. When the House of Lords passes a judgment in a case, it has to be followed by all courts if the case they are hearing is similar, whereas judgments of other courts are merely persuasive and do not need to be followed.

c. When a court gives a decision in a case, any courts of an equal or lower status have to follow it if the case they are hearing is similar, with no exception.

d. When the House of Lords or Court of Appeal hand down a judgment in a case, all other courts have to follow it if the case they are trying is similar, whereas the verdicts of all other courts are merely persuasive and do not need to be followed.

12) Of the following statements which is the best description of the Treaties underpinning the European Community?

a. These treaties are considered primary sources of EU law but only have direct effect when incorporated in the law of Member States.

b. These treaties are primary sources of EU law and have direct effect.

c. These treaties are not binding, merely providing guidance, advice or examples of good practice.

d. These treaties constitute part of the secondary legislation of the EU enshrined in Article 249 and are both directly applicable and directly effective.

13) Which of the following is a binding 'order' that is issued by one of the institutions of the European Union and is addressed to a state or an individual?

    a. A regulation ᷄

    b. An opinion

    c. A decision

    d. A recommendation

14) Which of the following most accurately describes the purposive rule in relation to statutory interpretation?

    a. Examining the social and economic context of the Act.

    b. Giving words used in a statute their ordinary, plain and natural meaning.

    c. Applying common sense if giving words within a statute their ordinary, plain and natural meaning would lead to absurdity. ·

    d. Examining the original purpose of the particular provision under consideration.

15) Courts have the power to state that a piece of primary legislation does not comply with a Convention [European Convention on Human Rights] right. What is the effect of such a statement?

    a. It corrects the incompatible legislation in question.

    b. It informs the government that the legislation is not 'Convention compliant' and no longer implements the legislation.

    c. It notifies the government that the legislation is not 'Convention compliant', but the legislation in question remains in force. ·

    d. The primary legislation is repealed.

16) What general principles does the European Court of Human Rights follow to delineate the boundaries of state liability and individual rights?

    a. Equitable principles

    b. 'Margin of appreciation' and equity

    c. 'Margin of appreciation', proportionality and equity

    d. 'Margin of appreciation', and proportionality .

17) Which of the following statements are correct? (More than one option may be selected)

    a. In criminal court cases the requirement concerning proof is beyond reasonable doubt. .

    b. In criminal court cases the degree of evidence sought is on the balance of probabilities.

    c. In criminal court cases it is usually up to the prosecution to prove an allegation. ,

    d. Criminal law is part of public law. ,

18) Which of the following statements are correct? (More than one option may be selected)

    a. The individual who launches a civil action is referred to as the claimant. .

    b. In civil law the burden of proof is on the balance of probabilities.

    c. Civil law is part of private law. '

    d. In civil law the standard of proof is beyond reasonable doubt.

19) Which of the following statements are incorrect? (More than one option may be selected)

    a. A Directive is completely binding as a whole in all Member States and is directly applicable. ,

    b. If it wishes to, a Member State can opt not to apply a Directive if it considers its implementation inappropriate.

    c. A Directive is not binding on Member States.

    d. A Directive grants some leeway to Member States as to how to the Directive is implemented in the Member State's domestic law. .

20) Which one of the following is a binding order that is issued by one of the institutions of the European Union and is addressed to a State or an individual?

    a. A decision

    b. An opinion

    c. A Directive

    d. A Regulation

21) Which of these statements are accurate? (More than one option may be selected)

    a.   The Committee stage follows the second reading.

    b.   A bill may be introduced to either the House of Commons or the House of Lords.

    c.   The first reading is just a formal stage where only the title of the bill is read out. .

    d.   A bill can only be set in motion in the House of Commons.,

22) Which of the statements below best describes the objective of the second reading of a bill?

    a.   It is a time when Parliament can debate a bill in detail.

    b.   It is a chance for Parliament to debate the main principal of a bill. •

    c.   It is a time when Parliament can debate amendments added to the bill by the other chamber.

    d.   It is a chance for Parliament to debate changes that occurred at the Committee stage.

23) Which of the following statements are correct? (More than one option may be selected)

    a.   A judgment given by a single High Court judge is binding for other single High Court judges.

    b.   The Criminal Division of the Court of Appeal has more leeway to differ from previous judgments of its own than the Civil Division.

    c.   A statement made by a judge in the Supreme Court that is not part of the ratio decidendi of the case, but part of a majority verdict, is binding for lower courts.

    d.   When the Judicial Committee of the Privy Council deals with an appeal from a Commonwealth country, its advice has persuasive authority for English courts and can be binding in some circumstances.

24) Which of the following are types of public law? (More than one option may be selected)

    a.   Tort Law

    b.   Company Law

    c.   Administrative Law ·

    d.   Immigration Law ·

25) Which of the following are types of private law? (More than one option may be selected)

    a. Tort Law.
    b. Company Law.
    c. Criminal Law
    d. Administrative Law

Civil and Criminal Justice System

1) Bill has a claim against *Gossip!* magazine for the publication of defamatory material. His claim is estimated to be worth £18,000.

Please indicate which court this claim should be commenced in, and to which case management track the case is likely to be allocated.

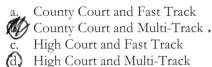

    a. County Court and Fast Track
    b. County Court and Multi-Track .
    c. High Court and Fast Track
    d. High Court and Multi-Track

2) The Civil Procedure Rules govern all proceedings in...

    a. The County Courts, the High Court and the Court of Appeal (Civil Division)
    b. The Crown Courts, the High Court and all divisions of the Court of Appeal
    c. The County Courts, the High Court and the Court of Appeal (Civil Division) and the Supreme Court
    d. The County Courts, the High Court and all divisions of the Court of Appeal

3) What is the outcome if the Magistrates' Court concludes it has jurisdiction to hear a criminal case when the defendant has been charged with an either-way offence?

    a. The defendant has the option of summary trial in the Crown Court or trial on indictment in the Magistrates' Court.
    b. The prosecution has the option of deciding if the defendant should face summary trial in the Crown Court or trial on indictment in the Magistrates' Court.
    c. The defendant has the freedom to choose whether to face summary trial in the Magistrates' court or trial by indictment in the Crown Court.
    d. It is up to the prosecution to decide whether the defendant should face summary trial in the Magistrates' court or trial by indictment in the Crown Court.

4) Would the following clause be considered a valid arbitration agreement according to the Arbitration Act 1996?

"All disagreements relating to this contract must be submitted to arbitration for determination."

a. Yes.
b. No

5) In an arbitration, the parties are known as...

a. Claimant and Respondent
b. Claimant and Defendant
c. Plaintiff and Respondent
d. Plaintiff and Defendant

6) James and Anna reside in properties next to each other. They are at present in dispute over where the boundary lies between their plots of land. Neither James nor Anna wish to leave their homes, and James is very frustrated with the dispute and is considering taking action.

Which of the types of action listed below do you consider would be appropriate in this situation?

a. Litigation
b. Arbitration
c. Early Neutral Evaluation
d. Mediation

7) Which of the following would NOT be strictly binding on a High Court judge?

a. A decision of the House of Lords
b. A decision of the Court of Appeal
c. A decision of a Divisional Court
d. A decision of the Privy Council

8) Of the powers listed below, which is NOT part of the civil jurisdiction of the Magistrates' Court?

a. The authority to issue a license to sell alcohol.
b. The authority to hand down orders in divorce hearings.
c. The authority to issue a maintenance order in line with the Children Act.
d. The authority to issue an order for the recovery of water charges.

9) Which of the following is NOT possible?

a. An appeal from the Magistrates' Court directly to the Divisional Court
b. An appeal from the Crown Court directly to the House of Lords
c. An appeal from the Divisional Court directly to the House of Lords
d. An appeal from the County Court directly to the Court of Appeal

10) What are the maximum sentencing powers of the Magistrates' Court for a single offence?

a. 12 months imprisonment and / or a fine of up to £5,000
b. 9 months imprisonment and / or a fine of up to £10,000
c. 6 months imprisonment and / or a fine of up to £5,000
d. 6 months imprisonment and / or a fine of up to £10,000

11) Of the options listed below which is the most accurate definition of the process of a case heard by the Queen's Bench Division of the High Court?

a. An appeal by the prosecution from the Magistrates' Court on a point of law.
b. An appeal by the defendant or the prosecution against a decision in the Crown Court.
c. An appeal by the defendant or the prosecution from the Magistrates' Court on a point of law.
d. An appeal from a county court on a question of law.

12) Which of the following statements is true?

a. A leapfrog appeal is an appeal from the High Court to the Supreme Court.
b. A leapfrog appeal is an appeal from the County Court to the Court of Appeal.
c. A leapfrog appeal is an appeal from the Crown Court to the Court of Appeal.
d. A leapfrog appeal is an appeal from the Magistrates' Court to the Queen's Bench Division of the High Court.

13) Appeals from the Crown Court involving a trial on indictment go to which court?

a. The Supreme Court
b. The Court of Appeal (Criminal Division)
c. The Queen's Bench Division of the High Court
d. The Queen's Bench Divisional Court

14) Which Act established the Supreme Court?

a. The Constitutional Reform Act 2005
b. The Constitutional Reform Act 2009
c. The Courts Act 2009
d. The Supreme Court Act 2009

15) How many divisions are there in the Court of Appeal?

a. One
b. Two
c. Three
d. Four

16) How many divisions are there in the High Court?

a. One
b. Two
c. Three
d. Four

17) Which of the following courts deal with criminal cases? (More than one option may be selected)

a. The County Court
b. The Magistrates' Court
c. The High Court
d. The Crown Court

18) Which one of the following courts deals with judicial review cases?

a. The High Court
b. The County Court
c. The Crown Court
d. The Court of Appeal (Criminal Division)

19) An action on the case was:

a. An action for a standard amount of money in return for a promise being honoured.
b. An action for the return of a particular piece of personal property wrongfully taken.
c. Used to provide a remedy where none was provided by a known common law action.

d.   An action for compensation following the violation of a person's sworn promise, by deed.

20) Which courts presently constitute the Supreme Court of Judicature?

a.   Supreme Court, Court of Appeal, High Court and Crown Court
b.   Supreme Court, Court of Appeal, High Court and County Court
c.   Court of Appeal, High Court, Crown Court
d.   Court of Appeal, High Court, County Court

21) The High Court is divided into which three divisions?

a.   Queen's Bench, Chancery, Family•
b.   Queen's Bench, Chancery, Admiralty
c.   Queen's Bench, Chancery, Probate
d.   Queen's Bench, Chancery, Equity

22) Of the statements below regarding the County Court which is NOT accurate?

a.   The judge who usually hears cases in the County Court is the Circuit judge.
b.   The Crown hears advice from the Lord Chancellor (following a fair and open competition administered by the Judicial Appointments Commission) before appointing Circuit judges and District judges.
c.   The County Court is the court that deals with the most civil cases.
d.   The County Court has limited jurisdiction as regards the Admiralty.

23) The personal injury small claims procedure involves claims of less than:

a.   £1,000 '
b.   £5,000
c.   £7,500
b.   £10,000

24) Which of the following is NOT a civil wrong?

a.   A wrongful act which is criminal. '
b.   A deliberate breach of contract.
c.   A breach of a fiduciary obligation.
d.   A breach of a tortious duty of care.

25) **Which of the following statements about the civil court structure is NOT accurate?**

    a. The Master of the Rolls is President of the Civil Division of the Court of Appeal.

    b. The Court of Appeal generally sits as six judges.

    c. The Probate, Divorce and Admiralty Division of the High Court were together because of their foundation in Roman and Canon Law.

    d. The Lord Chief Justice is President of the Criminal Division of the Court of Appeal.

26) **Which of the following statements about the civil court structure is accurate?**

    a. The Crown Court, Court of Appeal and the Supreme Court make up the Supreme Court of Judicature.

    b. The High Court, Court of Appeal and the Supreme Court make up the Supreme Court of Judicature.

    c. The Court of Appeal and the Supreme Court make up the Supreme Court of Judicature.

    d. The County Court, High Court and Court of Appeal make up the Supreme Court of Judicature.

27) **Which one of the following statements about the role of lay people in civil proceedings is NOT accurate?**

    a. Juries may be empanelled in defamation cases.

    b. Juries may be empanelled in coroner's courts.

    c. Lay people are often members of tribunal panels.

    d. Juries are regularly empanelled in personal injury cases.

28) **What is the standard of proof in civil matters?**

    a. Balance of convenience

    b. Balance of probabilities ⌐

    c. Balance of possibilities

    d. Balance of circumstances

29) **What is the standard of proof in criminal matters?**

    a. Beyond reasonable doubt -

    b. Beyond all reasonable doubt

    c. Beyond probable doubt

    d. Beyond possible doubt

30) Which of the following are methods of Alternative Dispute Resolution:

    i.   Litigation.
    ii. Mediation.
    iii. Arbitration.
    iv. A civil claim.

    a. i, ii and iv
    b. i and iii
    c. ii and iii .
    d. ii, iii and iv

Legal Professionals in the English Legal System

1) Helen is 24 years old and for the last four years has resided in Germany with her parents. She does not have a criminal record and has never had a mental illness.

Is Helen eligible to perform jury service?
    a. Yes, as long as she is on the electoral register.
    b. Yes, she is eligible regardless of whether she is on the electoral register.
    c. No, she does not own a property.
    d. No, she has been absent from the UK for too long.

2) It is now possible for a solicitor to qualify as a solicitor-advocate. This means that the solicitor will have rights of audience…
    a. in all courts.
    b. in all courts, except the Supreme Court.
    c. in all courts, except the Court of Appeal (Civil Division) and the Supreme Court.
    d. in all courts, except the Court of Appeal (all divisions) and the Supreme Court.

3) The Lord Chief Justice is …
    a. The new name for the Lord Chancellor.
    b. Head of the Judiciary in England and Wales.
    c. Chancellor of the High Court.
    d. President of the Queen's Bench Division.

4) James works as a solicitor for Oakfield Solicitors LLP. The Maxwell family is one of his oldest and most significant clients, as he has dealt with them for 15 years. The Maxwell's youngest daughter, Leyanda, has been detained after hitting her boyfriend in the street. From the police station, Leyanda called her father. Straight after receiving the call from his daughter, Mr Maxwell called James and asked him to represent Leyanda.

Can James represent Leyanda?
    a.   Yes. As Leyanda's father instructed James, he can act.
    b.   Yes, but only on condition Leyanda agrees with her father's instructions.
    c.   Yes. James, as the family's solicitor, is the only solicitor authorised to act for Leyanda.
    d.   No. Issues of conflict may arise as James has acted previously on behalf of other family members.

5) Which of the following would you NOT expect to find sitting in the Court of Appeal (Criminal Division)?

    a.   The Lord Chief Justice
    b.   A Lord Justice of Appeal
    c.   A Circuit Judge
    d.   A High Court Judge

6) A judge is listed as 'Maxwell J' in a judgment. How should this be said?

    a.   Judge Maxwell
    b.   Mister Justice Maxwell
    c.   Justice Maxwell
    d.   Sir Anthony Maxwell

7) A judge is listed as 'Queen LJ' in a judgment. How should this be said?

    a.   Sir Queen
    b.   Lord Queen
    c.   Lord Justice Queen
    d.   Mister Justice Queen

8) Which of the following are acceptable jury verdicts?

i. A unanimous verdict of 'guilty'.
ii. A 'guilty' verdict by a majority of 9 – 3 after three hours of deliberation.
iii. A 'guilty' verdict by a majority of 11 – 1 after two hours of deliberation.
iv. A 'guilty' verdict by a majority of 10 – 2 after four hours of deliberation.

a. i and iv
b. ii, iii and iv
c. i, iii and iv
d. All of the above

9) Of the following, which title does NOT exist as a judicial office in England and Wales?

a. The Lord Chief Justice
b. The Master of the Rolls
c. The President of the Family Division
d. Procurator Fiscal

10) What does 'P' stand for?

a. The Lord Chancellor
b. The Master of the Rolls
c. P – President (Head of Family Division and a President head of QBD) .
d. The Lord Chief Justice

11) What are the judges in the Supreme Court called?

a. Law Lords ·
b. Master of the Rolls
c. Lord Chief Justice
d. Lord Chancellor

12) The four Inns of Court are:

a. Lincoln's Inn, Middle Temple, Inner Temple and Clifford's Inn
b. Lincoln's Inn, Middle Temple, Inner Temple and Barnard's Inn
c. Lincoln's Inn, Middle Temple, Inner Temple and Staples' Inn
d. Lincoln's Inn, Middle Temple, Inner Temple and Gray's Inn .

13) **Which of the following is the official title of those judges commonly referred to as Law Lords?**

    a. A judge at the County Court
    b. A judge at the Crown Court
    c. A judge at the High Court
    d. A judge at the Supreme Court

14) **Which of the following is NOT part of the role of the Lord Chancellor?**

    a.   A member of the Cabinet
    b.   Head the Ministry of Justice as the Secretary of State for Justice
    c.   Head of the Church of England
    d.   Recommendation of Queen's Counsel with the support of the selection panel

15) **Which of the following is a representative institution of solicitors?**

    a.   The Bar Standards Board
    b.   The Bar Council
    c.   Solicitors Regulation Authority
    d.   The Law Society

16) **Which of the following statements about trial by jury is NOT accurate?**

    a.   A jury consists of a panel of lay persons.
    b.   A jury is generally made up of 12 jurors, although it is possible for it to function with fewer than 12.
    c.   To qualify as a juror, there is a minimum income requirement.
    d.   Although juries usually hear criminal trials on indictment, sometimes a jury may deal with a civil matter.

17) **Prior to April 1999, the claimant in civil proceedings was known as:**

    a.   The pursuer
    b.   The litigator
    c.   The plaintiff
    d.   The litigant in person

18) The person against whom a civil action is brought is known as:

a. The accused
b. The prosecutor
c.) The respondent
d. The plaintiff

19) The judge who generally sits in the County Court is known as:

a. Puisne Judge
b. Recorder
c. Assistant Recorder
d.) Circuit Judge ⸗

20) Which one of the following is correct?

a. In employment tribunals only solicitors are permitted to represent clients.
b. In employment tribunals only barristers are permitted to represent clients.
c. Clients in employment tribunals may be represented by both solicitors and barristers.
d. Neither solicitors nor barristers can represent clients in employment tribunals.

ANSWERS

Source of Law (Domestic Legislation, Case Law and International Law)

1) c; 2) a; 3-) b; 4) b; 5) b; 6) a; 7) c; 8) b; 9) c; 10) b; 11) a; 12) b; 13) c; 14) a; 15) c; 16) d; 17) a, c, d; 18) a, c; 19) a, b, c; 20) a; 21) a, b, c; 22) b; 23) b, d; 24) c, d; 25) a, b → 16/25

Civil and Criminal Justice System

1) c; 2) a; 3-) c; 4) b; 5) a; 6) d; 7) d; 8) b; 9) b; 10) c; 11) c; 12) a; 13) b; 14) a; 15) b; 16) c; 17) b, c, d; 18) a; 19) c; 20) a; 21) a; 22) c; 23) a; 24) a; 25) b; 26) b; 27) d; 28) b; 29) a; 30) c

Legal Professionals in the English Legal System

1) a; 2) a; 3-) b; 4) b; 5) c; 6) b; 7) c; 8) a; 9) d; 10) c; 11) a; 12) d; 13) d; 14) c; 15) d; 16) c; 17) c; 18) c; 19) d; 20) c

14/20

103

GLOSSARY OF LEGAL TERMINOLOGY[1]

A

Accused	The person charged with a criminal offence.
Acquittal	Discharge of defendant following verdict or direction of not guilty.
Act	Legislation; Act of Parliament.
Actus reus	Guilty act.
Ad idem	Of the same mind. Sometimes read in contract law as *consensus ad idem* (meeting of minds).
Adjournment	Temporary suspension of legal proceedings.
Advocate	General term for a barrister or solicitor who represents a party at Court.
Affidavit	A sworn statement in writing made under oath or affirmed to be true and taken before an authorised person.

Affirmanti non neganti incumbit probation The burden of proof is on the claimant, not the person who denies the claim.

Affirmation	A statement by a witness who either has no religious belief, or whose religious beliefs do not allow them to swear the oath, that their testimony is true.
Affirmed	Indicates that a court has agreed with the decision of a lower court in respect of the same case.

Alternative Dispute Resolution An alternative method for parties to resolve dispute between parties (claimant and respondent).

Amicus Curiae	Literally, a friend of the Court, who is not a party to the case and uses their expertise to expound an independent view when asked by the Court.
Appeal	Application to a higher court for review of a decision of a lower court.
Appellant	Party who appeals.

---

[1] BPP, pp. 80-90.

Applied   Signifies that a court deems itself bound by a precedent, and is consequently following the same reasoning in the current case.

Approved   Means that a higher court declares that another case resolved by a lower court was dealt with properly.

Attorney-General The principal law officer of the Crown.

Audi alterem partem Hear the other side.

Award   The amount of damages assessed by the court.

B

Bail   A defendant's release from custody until the subsequent hearing of their case in Court. Bail is often granted conditional on a security being pledged or with conditions.

Balance of Probabilities The civil burden of proof.

Bankrupt   If someone is unable to pay debts to creditors and has all property administered by a liquidator or trustee and sold to pay their creditors, they are bankrupt. This is a consequence of an order under the Insolvency Act 1986.

Bar   Collective name for barristers.

Barrister   A member of the Bar.

Beyond Reasonable Doubt The criminal burden of proof.

Bona fide   In good faith.

Brief   A written document drawn up by a solicitor for a counsel who will represent a client at a hearing. The document should lay out the facts of the case and cite relevant jurisprudence.

Burden of proof   The duty of proving one's case. See *onus probandi*.

C

Caution   (i) A warning administered by a Police Officer in place of a charge.

                       (ii) A warning administered by a Police Officer to an

individual being charged with an offence.

(iii) A notification made to the Land Registry by any individual who has an interest in a particular piece of land to make sure that nothing happens to the land without their knowledge.

Caveat emptor   Let the buyer beware.

Chambers   (i) Private room, or Court from which the public are excluded in which a District Judge or Judge may conduct certain sorts of hearings.

(ii) Offices used by a barrister.

Chancellor of the High Court Head of Chancery Division of the High Court

Chancery Division Division of the High Court which deals with company and commercial matters.

Charge   A formal accusation against a person that a criminal offence has been committed.

Chattel   Name given in law to personal property.

Chose   A thing.

Chose in action   A property right of a person which can only be recovered by action.

Circuit judge   A judge who sits in the County Court and/or the Crown Court.

Civil   Matters concerning individuals and not the State.

Civil system   System of jurisdiction derived from Roman law as opposed to common law systems.

Claimant   Party issuing a claim. Previously known as the plaintiff.

Committal   (i) Committal Order: A Court document sending a person to prison.

(ii) Committal for Sentence: If the Magistrates are of the opinion that the offence deserves a greater sentence than they are able to hand down, they may refer the defendant to the Crown Court for sentencing by a judge.

(iii) Committal for Trial: After Magistrates have examined a case which is indictable or an either way offence, the referring of the case to the Crown Court.

Common law   (i) Law established by judgments. Distinguished from a civil system.

(ii) Law derived from the jurisdiction of the common law courts as opposed to the Court of Chancery.

Compensation   Sums of money which provide recompense for loss suffered by an individual.

Considered   Used where a court discusses a reported case, but has not reached a conclusion as to its application.

Contempt of court Disobedience of the judicial process.

Contributory negligence   When a party is partially responsible for the injury they suffer. If courts decide there has been contributory negligence the damages awarded to the claimant may be reduced. See Law Reform (Contributory Negligence) Act 1945.

Corroboration   Evidence of one person confirming that of another.

Counsel   Barrister.

Counterclaim   A claim made by a defendant against a claimant in an action.

County Court   County Courts are responsible for civil matters, including all small claims by creditors up to £15,000.

Court   Body with judicial authority.

Court of Appeal   Divided into: (i) civil and (ii) criminal divisions. It hears appeals from decisions of the High Court and County Courts, and against convictions or sentences passed by the Crown Court.

Creditor   A person to whom money is owed by a debtor.

Criminal   Person found guilty of a criminal offence.

Crown Court   Crown Courts handle offences referred to them for trial by Magistrates Courts. Cases in a Crown Court take place with a judge and jury. The Crown Court is also an appeal Court for cases initially dealt with by Magistrates. Crown Courts are also able to hear certain civil and family cases.

Curia advisari vult The court took time. This tag usually appears in a law report in the truncated form *cur adv vult*. This means that after hearing the case the court took time to deliberate before announcing its judgment.

D

Damages   A sum of money claimed as compensation for a wrong occasioned.

De facto   In fact.

De jure   By right.

De minimis non curat lex The law takes no account of trifling matters.

Debtor   Person owing money to a creditor.

Declaration   Court order setting out the rights of a party.

Default judgement Obtained by the claimant as a result of the failure of a defendant to comply with the requirements of a claim.

Defendant   (i) person sued in civil matters;

(ii) person standing trial or appearing for sentence in criminal matters.

Distinguished   A term used when a court does not want to follow precedent in an earlier case, but is obliged to do so on account of the doctrine of *stare decisis*.

District judge   A judge who works in a County Court or Magistrates Court and deals with a wide range of applications, proceedings and final hearings.

Divisional Court   As well as having an original jurisdiction of their own, all three divisions of the High Court have appellate jurisdiction to hear appeals from lower Courts and tribunals. The Divisional Court of the Chancery Division deals with appeals in bankruptcy matters from the County Court. The Divisional Court of the Queen's Bench Division deals largely with certain appeals on points of law from many Courts. The Divisional Court of the Family Division deals largely with appeals from Magistrates Courts in matrimonial matters a 'next friend' or 'guardian *ad litem*'.

Dock   Place for the defendant in a criminal court.

Doli incapax   Incapable of crime.

E

Either way offence A type of offence where the accused has the choice of opting either for the case to be heard by magistrates or to be heard in front of a jury in the Crown Court.

Equity   Body of legal principles developed by the Court of Chancery.

Ex parte   By a party. An *ex parte* application is made by one party. They are now known as without notice applications.

Expressio Unius est Exclusio Alterius When one or more things of a class are expressly mentioned, others of the same class are excluded.

Ex turpi causa non oritur action No right of action arises from a base cause

Examination in chief Examination of a witness by the person who calls him.

Executor   A person(s) specified to carry out the terms of a will.

F

Family Division Division of the High Court which deals with family matters such as divorce or wardship.

G

Garnishee   A court order by a claimant for money or other assets belonging to the defendant to be paid to the claimant.

Guarantor   A person who agrees to be responsible for the debts of another person if that person fails to make the repayments on a loan as agreed.

H

Habeas Corpus   Produce the body. A writ commanding that a person held in custody be produced before the court.

Head of Criminal Justice Formerly held by the Lord Chief Justice, but created as a separate post following changes to the role by the CRA 2005.

High Court A Civil Court which consists of three divisions:

   i.   Queen's Bench (can be known as King's Bench Division if a King is assuming the throne) - civil disputes for recovery of money, including breach of contract, personal injuries, libel/slander;

   ii.   Family - concerned with matrimonial matters and proceedings relating to children;

   iii.   Chancery - property matters including fraud and bankruptcy.

House of Lords Previously the highest court in the UK.

I

Ignoratia juris non excusat Ignorance of the law is no excuse.

In camera   In the chamber. An *in camera* hearing is held in private.

In curia   In open court.

In limine   On the threshold. An *in limine* objection is a preliminary objection.

In loco parentis   In place of a parent.

In personam   Against the person.

In rem   Against the matter. Proceedings directed against property as opposed to an individual.

Indictable offence A criminal offence triable only by the Crown Court.

Injunction   An order issued by a Court, usually to prevent a person or persons from a particular act, or to stipulate compliance. In the event that the order is ignored, a contempt of court has occurred.

Inns of Court   Lincoln's Inn, Inner Temple, Middle Temple, Gray's Inn. They have the privilege of granting the status or degree of barrister.

Inter vivos   Between living persons.

Interlocutory	Interim, pending a full order/decision.
Intestate	To die without a will.
Intra vires	Within the powers.
Issue	To initiate civil proceedings.

J

Judge	Officer appointed to administer court proceedings.
Judgment	Final decision of a court.
Juror	A person summoned to court to be part of a jury.
Jury	Body of lay persons convened to hear a criminal (though sometimes a civil) matter. A jury consists of 12 jurors.

Justice of the Peace A lay Magistrate.

Jurisdiction	The area over which a court has legal authority.

L

Law Lords	Describes the judges who sit on the Supreme Court.
Lien	A legal right to withhold goods/property of another until payment is made.
Litigation	Legal proceedings.
Locus in quo	The place in which.
Long Vacation	Period between 1st August and 30th September when the High Court only hears urgent matters.
Lord Chancellor	The cabinet minister responsible for the Ministry of Justice.

Lord Chief Justice The head of the Judiciary in England and Wales.

Lord Justice of Appeal Title given to certain of the judges who sit in the Court of Appeal.

Lord of Appeal in Ordinary Official title of a Law Lord.

Lords Spiritual	Those bishops holding seats in the House of Lords.

The Archbishops of Canterbury and York, the Bishops of London, Durham and Winchester and twenty-one other bishops.

Lords Temporal   The peers of the realm with seats in the House of Lords, other than the Lords Spiritual.

M

Magistrates' Court A Court where criminal cases are heard by justices of the peace who examine evidence and either pass judgment themselves or refer to the Crown Court for trial or sentence. Magistrates' Courts also have jurisdiction in a broad spectrum of civil matters.

Master   Judicial officer of the High Court in the Royal Courts of Justice who normally deals with preliminary matters before trial.

Master of the Rolls Senior civil judge in the Court of Appeal.

Material facts   A fact on which the outcome of the case depended.

Mens rea   Guilty mind.

Mitigation   (i) Reasons for lessening a sentence which might be imposed in criminal matters.

(ii) In civil law it refers to limiting one's losses after an act.

Mortgagee   The creditor in whose favour a mortgage is created.

Mortgagor   The debtor who creates a mortgage.

N

Nemo agit in se ipsum No one brings legal proceedings against himself.

Nemo dat quod non habet No one can give that which he has not.

Nemo debet judex esse in causa sua propria No one ought to be a Judge in his own cause.

Non est factum   This is not my deed.

Noscitur a sociis A court will examine words in the context of the Act in its entirety.

Notary Public A person with the authority to swear oaths and authenticate documents.

O

Oath A verbal promise by a person with religious beliefs to tell the truth.

Obiter dictum Things said by the way. Part of a judgement that is not crucial for the decision but remarked upon by the judge. Such remarks are not binding.

Official Solicitor An official can represent and act for people who are unable to represent themselves, such as children or persons with mental problems. Official solicitors are appointed by the Lord Chancellor.

Onus probandi Burden of proof.

Order Direction of the court.

Overruled Used when a court declares a decision has been superseded and is not correct.

P

Pari passu On an equal footing.

Parol Anything done by word of mouth.

Per curiam By the Court. An expression indicating that a decision was arrived at by the Court.

Personal Application An application made to the Court by an individual without legal representation.

Plaintiff Formerly a person initiating civil legal proceedings. Now known as a claimant.

Precedent A judgment which establishes principles or rules of law that become a guide for subsequent similar cases.

President of the Family Division Senior judge in the Family Division of the High Court.

President of the Queen's Bench Division Senior judge of the Queen's Bench Division of the High Court.

Probate   Legal recognition of the validity of a will.

Prosecution   The institution or conduct of criminal proceedings against a person.

Puisne judge   (pronounced *puny*) High Court judge (except the heads of each division). Puisne means junior and is used to distinguish High Court judges from senior judges at the Court of Appeal.

Q

Quash   To declare something is no longer valid.

Quasi   As if.

Quantum   The amount of a claim for damages which is determined by the court.

Queen's Bench Division Division of the High Court which deals with contract disputes and other matters not dealt with in the other Divisions.

Queen's Counsel Barristers of at least ten years standing may apply to become Queen's Counsel (QCs). QCs take on important cases and are colloquially called 'silks' on account of the gown they wear. If the monarch is a king they are referred to as King's Counsel.

R

Ratio decidendi Reasons for the decision. This is a proposition of law which is necessary for the decision in the case. The opposite of obiter dictum.

Recorder   Members of the legal profession (barristers or solicitors) who are appointed to act in a judicial capacity on a part time basis.

Res ipsa loquitur The thing speaks for itself.

Res judicata   A thing adjudged.

Respondent	In a court case the person whom a petition is made against. Also, on an appeal, the party apart from an appellant against whom an appeal is lodged.
Reversed	A higher court has determined that the decision of the lower court in the same case was wrong.
Right of audience	The right to appear in a Court and conduct proceedings on behalf of another person.

S

Senior Courts	Collective name of the Crown Court, High Court, DivisionalCourts and Court of Appeal, and The Supreme Court.
Silk	Alternative term used for a Queen's Counsel, because of the material used to make their gowns.
Solicitor	Member of the legal profession chiefly concerned with advising clients and preparing their cases.
Stare decisis	It is also known as the doctrine of precedent.
Statutory Instrument	A document issued by the relevant authority (generally a Government Minister or committee) denoted in an Act of Parliament amending the original Act.
Stipendiary Magistrate	Legally qualified and salaried Magistrate.
Sub judice	In the course of trial. A matter which is sub judice is being considered by the court.
Subpoena	Summons ordering an individual to attend court to give evidence.
Sui juris	A person of full age (18) and of sound mind.
Summary judgement	Judgement obtained by a plaintiff where there is no defence to the case.
Summary offence	An offence triable only by the Magistrates' Court.
Summing-up	The judge's summary of the evidence heard by the court in a criminal case and relevant law prior to a jury retiring to deliberate over the verdict.
Supreme Court	Name of the highest court in the UK.

Supreme Court of Judicature Former name of the Senior Courts.

T

Testator   A person who makes a will.

U

Ultra vires   Beyond the powers.

V

Verdict   The finding of guilt or innocence made by a jury.

Vice-Chancellor   Former title of the Chancellor of the High Court.

Volenti non fit injuria No injury is done to a person who consents.

W

Will   A document detailing a distribution of assets on the maker's death.

Witness   A person who gives evidence at court.

RECOMMENDED READING LIST

Barnett, H., *Constitutional and Administrative Law*, 10th ed., Routledge, 2013

BPP Law School, *Study Notes on English Legal System*, BPP Law School, 2018.

Clinch, P., *Using a Law Library: A Student's Guide to Legal Research Skills*, 2nd ed., Blackstone Press, 2001.

Cockburn, T. and Shirley, M., *Nutshell: Equity,* 5th ed., Thomson Reuters (Lawbook Co), 2019.

Crick, B., *Democracy: A Very Short Introduction*, Oxford University Press, 2002.

Dane, J., Thomas, P.A., and Knowles, J., *How to Use a Law Library: An Introduction to Legal Research*, 4th ed., Sweet & Maxwell, 2001.

Dicey, A. V., *Introduction to the Study of the Law of Constitution*, Liberty Fund Inc., 2019.

Dreadon, K., 'Mediation Order', (2005) 149 SJ 12.

Elliott, C. and Quinn, F., *English Legal System*, 6th ed., Oxford University Press, 2015.

Gillespie, A. and Weare, S., *The English Legal System*, 5th ed., Oxford University Press, 2015.

Greenberg, D., *Craies on Legislation*, 11th ed., Sweet & Maxwell, 2016.

Harris, P.; Hurden, N. and the Constitutional and Administrative Law Team, *GDL & LLM Study Notes on Constitutional and Administrative Law*, BPP Law School, 2018.

Holland, J. and Webb, J., *Learning Legal Rules*, 9th ed., Oxford University Press, 2016.

Kelly, D., *Slapper and Kelly's The English Legal System*, 19th ed., Routledge, 2020.

McLeod, I., *Legal Method,* 9th ed., Palgrave Macmillan, 2013.

Thomas, M. and McGourlay, C., *Concentrate English Legal System*, Oxford University Press, 2017.

Wilson, S., Rutherford, H. & Storey, T., *English Legal System*, 2nd ed., Oxford University Press, 2016.

INDEX

Printed in Great Britain
by Amazon